THE
MISINTERPRETED
GOSPEL
OF SINGLENESS

THE MISINTERPRETED GOSPEL OF SINGLENESS

A cultural critique of myths surrounding singleness in the Christian community

KHRISTI ADAMS

ISBN: 1492765198
ISBN 13: 978-1492765196

TABLE OF CONTENTS

For Mom:

"Many women do noble things,
but you surpass them all."

Introduction

"It can be hard to stand straight in a crooked room."
— *Melissa Harris-Perry*

I recently heard a preacher speaking to his congregation about marriage and family. When he touched on the topic of singleness, he offered singles a stern warning. He said that single people need to stop being angry with God because they are single. He said that they should wait patiently and be careful not to rush into anything. While I wholeheartedly agreed with the later part of his teaching, something about the first part just didn't sit right with me. I agree that people should take a step back when being angry with God for any relationship realities they can't control. At the same time, when it comes to people who are single, I would argue that any apparent "anger with God" has been instigated by a negative message surrounding singleness in the Christian community. Perhaps single people wouldn't be as angry with God had they received messages of inclusion and acceptance from God's people, as opposed to the message that singleness is some form of a biblical plague. If the message had been communicated that the status of one's relationship didn't define his or her worth in the kingdom of God, then I truly believe that many people who are single would be a lot more at peace in their singleness. They would not feel their self-worth devalued because they weren't married. They would embrace spiritual, physical, and emotional wholeness and realize that the world needs who they are as individuals.

So there lies the problem: that celebration appears to reside only in those who join as one. Maybe there are no ceremonies or parties for people who are single. Regardless, I've realized that many find themselves more at the tail end of awkward jokes or caught in the middle of uncomfortable questions that seem more like interrogations, rather than being celebrated for who they are and loved, cherished, and embraced by the community around them. This is the misinterpreted gospel of singleness. It is, what I believe to be, a negative message, communicated to individuals over a period of time—often unintentionally—which causes them to adopt unhealthy views of themselves and their relationships. This gospel is not only preached from pulpits, but family, friends, random people on the street, and even pop culture would suggest that the true value of one's self can be discovered only within the context of a romantic relationship. This is not just something that I have perceived, but something I have lived. I will attempt to break down this ideology in this book, which is a critical approach to the misinterpreted teaching that I believe has done more harm than good.

As a single woman, it's only natural that my audience would target single women. However, I encourage men and people who are married, as well as people from other faith communities, to read this book so that they can possibly gain another perspective. At the same time, I can't speak on behalf of every single woman, but what I can do is speak from my own experience in hopes that there might be something in my story that will resonate with someone.

Chapter 1

THE MYTH OF
THE SINGLES MINISTRY

"You know, there's a ministry in the church for people like you."

Here I am, Sunday morning and in church—the one place I go where I can experience community and feel safe. Taking a seat in the left corner, I leave one open for another friend who I had decided to invite to church for the first time. Once she arrives, I brag to her about how amazing the church is and how I want for her to experience what I had in a community of great worship and teaching. As the service commences, music fills the atmosphere and the congregation of people dancing, singing, and lifting their hands brings me such joy. There is a feeling that we are all unified in a common purpose in spite of our differences of background.

Unfortunately, this sentiment doesn't last long when the pastor takes the pulpit shortly after announcements. He jokes about his "smokin' hot" wife and goes on and on about how he can't get much more blessed than this, having found "the one" at a young age and gotten married right away. He then proceeds to ask the congregation, "How many of you in the room are single?" I don't raise my hand, fearing the attention drawn to myself would only make things worse. As hands go up, one by one-the majority being college-aged students-he tells each person to look around the room. "Your future husband or wife may be here." Everyone in the congregation laughs. He then begins to attempt to "hook up" certain people in congregation with one another, playfully mentioning ones who would be good for the other. I creep lower and lower into my seat. My friend looks over at me in disgust and says, "What is this, a meat market? I am never coming back here again." I was so embarrassed and even more embarrassed that this was not the first time that I have had moments like this at many churches—in my lifetime.

I wonder if I'm the only person on earth who has ever felt totally uncomfortable when one of the leaders at a church makes single jokes. I thought about what Carrie Bradshaw once said in an episode of the HBO television show "Sex & the City." She said, "When did being single become the equivalent of being a modern-day leper?" Later in the service, the pastor mentions the marriage conference coming up, which is for those married or thinking about getting engaged. But no fear, if you are single, there is a ministry in the church for you too. It's called "the singles ministry." They do fun things like go bowling and have poetry nights, and sometimes there will even be a speaker who comes and tells them what they should be doing while they're "waiting." The singles ministry is a ministry whose purpose I've never quite understood. I believe a major reason for this is because most singles ministries do not have a clear understanding of their purpose or intent. Marriage ministries are designed to build successful marriages through marriage enrichment. They typically have clear strategies and programming in place to develop an effective ministry. Singles ministries, on the other hand, are not so clear-cut. I recently saw a mission statement for a singles ministry that said its purpose is "to orchestrate a **ministry** for **singles** to gather in worship, discipleship, fellowship, and outreach." Most singles ministries wind up being more reflective of a babysitters club than an actual strategic ministry: something to keep the singles busy while they're waiting. I believe a lot of this dilemma is not any fault of ministry leaders as much as a failure of the church at large in coming up with a comprehensive, holistic theology of singleness. Instead, we have preached a misinterpreted gospel of singleness.

The misinterpreted gospel of singleness is:

> *a negative message-oftentimes unintentional-communicated to individuals over a period of time that causes them to adopt unhealthy views of self and relationships.*

This is the message and unintentional energy that the Christian community has been sending to women and men. This message has been demonstrated in many forms and languages, which, over time, produce destructive ways of thinking and impulsive decision making by single individuals. Recently I had a conversation with an old friend whom I hadn't spoken with in a long time. This friend had spent the last eight years of her life applying to medical schools, just to get rejected each time. She had dreams of being a doctor her entire life and was determined to see that dream come true. She went back to get a master's degree in hopes that this degree would increase her chances of getting into medical school. She worked in positions that would add to her résumé to increase her chances of being accepted. Finally, her acceptance came. This was such an amazing testament and demonstration of her perseverance and strength. When we recently spoke, she was closing out her second year and was more stressed than usual. When I asked her how she was doing—aside from the stress of finals—she talked about how discontented she was with her relationship status. She stated that she'd been single for a few years now, and all she wanted to do was to get "wifed up." She said that she feared she would never get married because many women in her profession don't. As a single, thirty-year-old woman, she felt her time was running out. I reminded her that she was a strong, beautiful, and capable woman. I reminded her that there was no such thing as a deadline and that she need not fear. I reminded her that she had so much to contribute to this world, whether married or single. I could tell that my words made her feel better when she thanked me. I wondered why my words were such a rarity for her and why those messages reminding her of her worth were deficient in her life.

The Accumulation Theory

Although I single out the Christian community's influence when it comes to these harmful messages, I believe they come from many different channels. They come from family, friends, television, music, classrooms, and so on. Once these messages accumulate over time, they become ingrained within a person's psyche. When I was a student at Temple University, I majored in advertising. One of the things we learned in advertising was about the significance of product and message placement before potential consumers. The idea was to place a product or a message before an individual at least a thousand times each day, without that person realizing it. For example, if we advertise a particular brand of cereal in commercials, billboards on the highway, magazine ads, on the radio, and on some random person's T-shirt, then later on that night, when that individual begins to crave that brand of cereal, she thinks it was her idea. At the time we called it "the accumulation of minimal effects."

> **Accumulation Theory:** The view that the impact of any one message on any specific person may be minimal, but consistent, persistent, and corroborated messages result in minor changes among audiences that gradually add up over time to produce significant changes in society or culture.[i]

This accumulation theory applies to many things. In regards to the anti-single doctrine, it suggests that a negative message around singleness has accumulated in the hearts of men and women and caused damaging results. I, personally, am against systems that communicate harmful messages and push to establish them as normative. It's particularly difficult when one specific message has been so deeply ingrained within the psyche of our society and Christian culture. Even now, writing this book as a thirty-one-year-old single woman, I struggle with countering messages that have been communicated to me my entire life that suggest I should be married by now, and because I'm not, I have somehow failed. Furthermore, because I am not, I should be sitting and waiting for God to finally bless me and send me someone, when in reality God has already blessed me with a wonderful life, a wonderful community, and wonderful gifts and talents that I can use to make this world a better place. If at some point in my journey I meet someone who can partner with me in this life, then that too will be a wonderful blessing. But the idea that one life is greater than the other, or one has more significance than the other, is deception.

There Are No Singles

At a chapel service at Azusa Pacific University in 2011, Dr. Scott Daniels spoke on the topic of sexuality and addressed singleness with the following statement:

> We have to recover something like this: a call to single-ness. Jesus and Paul both had calls to singleness in their life for the sake of the kingdom. We have so been shaped by a romanticized view of love that almost everybody in this room, if you don't get married, will consider that some form of failure in your life.

I think when many people hear the phrase "a call to single-ness," it scares them, simply because it suggests that a person is called to potentially be alone for the rest of his or her life. That might be an extreme way of looking at it, but I think that's what people perceive when they hear the phrase "a call to singleness." It's not something that even I am shouting from the mountain-tops of something that I aspire to be called to. If most people were given the option of having to journey through this difficult, yet exciting, challenging, and wonderful life by themselves or with a partner, many of us would opt to partner with someone. So, a call to singleness isn't the most desired call, especially if you're looking at it through the lens of equating it to a call to be alone. Conversely, I don't believe that embracing a call to singleness means that you are called to go through life by yourself. It was Thomas Merton who wrote the book *No Man Is an Island*, which upholds the idea that no human being should live life as though he or she doesn't need anyone. It also suggests that no human being can fully experience life without the influence of community.

There is a movie that came out in 2007 called *Into the Wild* about a young man who graduates from college and decides that he no longer needs his family, his friends, or the support of any community around him. He believed that the truly peaceful and free life is one lived alone. He believed that these relationships were hindering him in that philosophy of life, so he decided that living in the wilderness would make him a better human being. This young man leaves everything behind, sells his belongings, says good-bye to his family, and embarks on a journey to find his place in this world, alone. What's most interesting about this three-hour movie is that along the way he meets people and finds himself in communities of individuals who embrace him. He establishes relationships each stop he makes. By the end of the movie, when he finally reaches his destination, it's not long before he realizes that life isn't meant to be journeyed alone, and unfortunately he learns that lesson the hard way.

Life is not meant to be journeyed alone. I do not believe that God intended for any of us to be isolated, no matter what our relationship status is. As human beings, we need each other. Therefore, a call to singleness could not possibly mean a call to being alone. This call to togetherness, I would argue, is not limited to romantic unions. My dear friend and coworker, Dr. Jamie Noling-Auth, wrote in her essay, "Singleness: More Than a Holding Pattern" that "within true Christian community, there are no singles. As 1 Corinthians 12 describes, we are the body. We are a family." She goes on to say "to assume that all singles should be relegated into a group where they should remain until they meet someone to legitimize their participation in the life of the congregation shows disregard for an important theological premise: God is the one who legitimizes our participation in the congregation, not a spouse or anyone else."[ii]

American Idol

Marriage has become an idol within the Christian community. The message is that you are not a significant part of this community unless you are joined to another person and, furthermore, you have offspring. In a recent conversation with a friend, I shared with him how content I was in my life at the moment, and he responded by saying, "Some women misinterpret temporary happiness with the ability to create their own personal utopia. Wrong. It's human to desire company and be in it. We're not meant to be alone." This response suggested what many in the Christian community believe: that the full extent of my contentment cannot be achieved until I am connected to another person in marriage.

In an article on marriage and singleness in *Christianity Today*, Katelyn Beaty writes:

> In subtle and not-so-subtle ways, perhaps local churches have acted as if monogamous sexual unions are the closest icon of heaven in this life. That no matter how much self-giving ministry or cultural creativity we undertake in our lifetimes, they are second-best without a spouse

> and children in tow…And so long as marriage ascends into the echelons of existential imperative—you must have *this* in order to be a complete human being—then my singleness becomes a problem.[iii]

She highlights the problematic equation that single equals incomplete and married equals complete: complete in happiness, complete in personhood, complete in calling. This belief is causing some single people to feel consigned as second-class citizens within a culture and within institutions supposedly built on being one in Christ. One of the most significant books giving an accurate view of singleness is Rodney Clapp's book *Families at the Crossroads*. Below are two quotes that highlight the singleness misconception within the Christian community:

> Frankly, most churches treat their singles ministry as little more than sanctified substitutes for singles bars. They see singles as peripheral to the core or central members, who belong to families. They assume that the "normal" single will sooner or later marry and start a family.[iv]

> We need to re-examine the reasons for seeing singleness as good so that, in a confused and searching postmodern world, we can reassert the goodness of singleness for the right reasons. Only so as we shall see, can we reinsert the

goodness of family, and the goodness of freedom, for the right reasons.[v]

He goes on to say that "one sure sign of a defective interpretation of Christian family is that it denigrates and dishonors singleness."[vi] Interestingly, this freedom that Clapp speaks of as an advantage, in traditional Christian thinking, is discouraged and looked down upon-especially among women.

While marriage is a special and celebrated union of two individuals, it has unfortunately become the Christian community's "golden calf."[vii] The core value of the church has been relegated to a single institution only. This exclusivity is in direct opposition to the message of Christ's kingdom that revolutionized family. It should not be "your family" but rather "our family." In Matthew 12:46-50, Jesus was talking to a crowd, and someone informed him that his mother and brothers were standing outside, waiting for him. In verse 48 Jesus replied to that person saying, "Who is my mother, and who are my brothers?" Pointing to his disciples, he said, "Here are my mother and my brothers. Whoever does the will of my Father in heaven is my brother and sister and mother." It was in this statement that Jesus reformed the family unit. He placed value in redefining traditional models of family and taught inclusiveness within the Kingdom of God. I've not only witnessed disunion when it comes to inclusion of singles but in many other areas as well. One example I've seen has been with children who need homes, whether through adoption or foster care. In spite of various plausible reasons why many are unable to foster or adopt, I've heard from those who are fully capable that "they want their *own* children." But to a follower of Christ, "their own" should take on a meaning unlike traditional ones. According to Christ, we all belong to each other.

In Luke 20, some of Jesus's dissenters approached him with a question. This was one of many questions that Jesus received from others who sought to catch him off guard.

> [28] "Teacher," they said, "Moses wrote for us that if a man's brother dies and leaves a wife but no children, the man must marry the widow and raise up offspring for his brother. [29] Now there were seven brothers. The first one married a woman and died childless. [30] The second [31] and then the third married her, and in the same way the seven died, leaving no children. [32] Finally, the woman died too. [33] Now then, at the resurrection whose wife will she be, since the seven were married to her?" [34] Jesus replied, "The people of this age marry and are given in marriage. [35] But those who are considered worthy of taking part in the age to come and in the resurrection from the dead will neither marry nor be given in marriage, [36] and they can no longer die; for they are like the angels."[viii]

I do not believe that Jesus was being anti-marriage with this statement. Jesus celebrated marriage unions and even used wedding banquet imagery in his parables. I believe in this passage, however, Jesus was refocusing their attention on what was important. This scripture speaks to the contemporary church as well, urging us to recenter our attention on the larger purpose of the kingdom of God. To put it lightly: stop idolizing marriage and turn your attention on things to come.

One Way to Look at It

What, then, is a call to singleness? I would argue that singleness is 1) a call to individual freedom, 2) a call to wholeness, 3) and a call to community.

A Call to Individual Freedom

> **in·di·vid·u·al·ism a.** Belief in the primary importance of the individual and in the virtues of self-reliance and personal independence.[ix]

Most people associate the phrase "individual freedom" with individualism. Individualism is often looked at in a negative light, especially in a world that thrives off of collective pressure. However, in this context, I would argue that living in individual freedom is necessary in one coming into his or her identity. It's important for a man or woman to understand what it means to make individual decisions. For example, it's important to understand what it means to budget on your own or pay your own bills.

It's important to have the freedom to travel to other states or countries while you have the opportunity to (not that you cannot with a family). It's important to discover likes and dislikes, to engage in new hobbies and things that help shape who you are as an individual. The idea is to be your authentic self before merging into a union with another individual. I know many couples who rushed into marriage before coming into the wholeness of self. They wanted so bad to learn everything about the other person that they failed to pay that same attention to themselves. They fought so hard to learn to love the other person that they had no idea what it meant to love themselves. As a result, years later they are struggling to understand who they are in their marriage, and it is suffering because of it. Self-discovery doesn't end when someone gets married, but I do believe that it is very helpful to a marriage when the individuals have had time to discover "self" before they get married. Our goal should be to discover our most authentic self, first. I have often heard people use phrases in relation to finding a partner in life like "I am looking for my other half." The other-half theory, while clever, is illusory thinking because a half is something that is incomplete, and one of the keys to a successful marriage is to be whole and complete *before* you get married. In the book of Genesis, when God created the man, God said that it is not good for the man to be alone.[x] It never says that God's creation in Adam was incomplete in any way. So instead of two halves equaling a whole, the idea is for two wholes to equal an even greater whole. You should be whole no matter your relationship status. You should be working on wholeness as a single person and wholeness as a married person.

A Call to Wholeness

May God himself, the God of peace, sanctify you through and through. May your whole <u>spirit, soul</u> and <u>body</u> be kept blameless at the coming of our Lord Jesus Christ. (1 Thess. 5:23)

It is additionally important to nurture, discipline, and focus on wholeness in all three areas that make up our being: spirit, soul, and body.

SPIRIT: Spiritual formation is essential to the lifestyle of faith-filled people. In engaging in spiritual care, space must be created to reflect, engage, challenge, and grow. Your commitment to maintaining spiritual wholeness is part of the development of the whole person. The ultimate goal is not redundancy but formation, and to be spiritually formed is to be transformed. We cannot afford to suffocate our spirits; therefore, our spiritual growth is a requirement for wholeness.

SOUL (mind, will, and emotions): The mind is constantly processing and taking in new information. Intentionally exposing yourself to new ways of thinking and education is also necessary to growth. Furthermore, making emotional and mental health a priority is just as essential. Whether it is in moments of reflective solitude or regular visits to a counselor, in a frenzied society, mental health has to take precedence.

BODY: I once saw a quote that said "Embrace and love your body. It is the most amazing thing you will ever own." This is so true. In fact, even scripture highlights it in Paul's letter to the church at Corinth:

> 1 Corinthians 6:19: Don't you realize that your body is the temple of the Holy Spirit, who lives in you and was given to you by God? You do not belong to yourself.

This scripture is often used in reference to sex, and even though we are sexual beings, the physical body is so much more. Body care includes taking in proper foods and regular exercise, which prevents poor health. No matter your genetic disposition or current weight, body care is not about dieting as much as it is about keeping your body in good repair.

A Call to Community

As I mentioned earlier, in Matthew 12 Jesus redefines traditional family concepts in a single encounter with a crowd:

> [46]While Jesus was still talking to the crowd, his mother and brothers stood outside, wanting to speak to him. [47] Someone told him, "Your mother and brothers are

standing outside, wanting to speak to you." [48] He replied to him, "Who is my mother, and who are my brothers?" [49] Pointing to his disciples, he said, "Here are my mother and my brothers. [50] For whoever does the will of my Father in heaven is my brother and sister and mother."

Here Jesus challenges the crowd by implying that his priority is with the entire body of believers. Within that entirety is his family. This was and still is a very radical way of thinking. Regrettably, the majority of Jesus's followers in contemporary Christian culture have yet to catch on. Jesus is redefining community. We have a responsibility to seek out and engage the community around us. We are called to redefine family, which includes learning how to love and live with one another. I once heard someone say that "if we're not fulfilling our callings, then the community suffers." There is a mutual dependence when it comes to community: community needs us as much as we need the community. Our strengths and aptitudes are to be used for the benefit of the community around us.

A Universal Call

It's time we realize that singleness is a universal call to everyone, because everyone at some point in his or her life will be single. The length of that season will vary, but we are all called to commit to freedom, wholeness, and community. I believe that if more people would commit to this call—to gleaning all they can from understanding their individuality—then we would have healthier marriages, mainly because we wouldn't have people entering into them, seeking another individual to "complete" them. They would have committed to individual wholeness prior. Singleness is a seasonal call for some, and for others it may be a call that extends beyond one particular season. A call to singleness is not a call to waiting, nor is it a call to loneliness, as it has often been projected in the Christian community. Because of our failure to communicate a healthy message and to accurately define what this call is, many people have been left wounded and insecure. However the message has been communicated, it is possible to be called to the life of discipleship as a single woman or man.

SINCERELY,
SECOND-CLASS CITIZEN

I grew up in an intentional Christian community that started during the Jesus Movement era of the late 60s/early 70s. This church goes by the name Jesus People USA Evangelical Covenant Church, located in uptown Chicago. It's a very non-standard Christian experience in that most of the hippie enclaves from the Jesus freak era have evaporated. What that meant is that I grew up simultaneously surrounded by a bunch of people who were following Jesus in an extremely purposeful way but most of whom did not have any experience with the church prior to their commitment to Jesus or people who had a negative experience prior. They felt their approach to Jesus needed to be intentional, and it affected every dimension of their lives. Secondly, because they didn't have a prior experience with church, they just had to go with what scripture would say and apply it to their lives as they read it. They didn't have the framework of theology of the traditional church informing their decisions. That had upsides and downsides. I had a very nonstandard experience of growing up in the church as it relates to sexual ethics and what it meant to be single. There was a lot of discussion about sexuality that was very healthy, which is not the case for people who grow up in a traditional church context. Because we didn't have the downside of tradition, initially it was still a very restrictive environment.

For a long time men and women barely talked to each other until they were engaged. It was their way of creating fail-safes. But for me, by the time I grew up, the culture shifted and had come to more of a middle ground. This affected my decisions and my way of thinking as I grew up.

In spite of this, I still wound up being exposed to the stereotypical second-class opinion with respect to anyone who was single. I remember encountering it most profoundly when I was at a church that had its own Christian private school. I didn't know 100 percent what I wanted to do after I graduated from high school, but I was pretty sure I wanted to go to college and teach mathematics. So I thought, why not kill a year teaching math first to really find out if that's what I want to do. I found that there was a need within the school, and I had accrued a lot of respect by the time I graduated. So I wound up teaching mathematics for a year. I was also involved with launching a number of ministries in the church in the time I had between working. These ministries were focused predominantly toward older teenagers and young adults. Despite the fact that I was involved with all these different ministries and was working a pretty challenging job-I was teaching second-, fifth-, ninth-, and eleventh-grade math-I still was not regarded as being as "adult" as people who got married right away. I remember at one point somebody making this comment about how I was really growing into being a great guy and that one of these days I would be an awesome man of God or something like that. I remember it hitting me as a backhanded compliment. Almost like, what more would I need to do in order for you to regard me as being someone who had fully arrived to adulthood? Around this time I started becoming more interested in my Jewish heritage (my dad is Jewish). Within Judaism we have a way of affirming one's full participation in community way before you're twenty-one or having kids. By the time you reach your bar mitzvah or bat mitzvah (if you're a woman), you are thirteen or fourteen years old and are able to definitively comment on the Torah and participate in the minyan.

So I remember that comment I heard as an adult in this Christian community striking me. It was such a weird thing to say to someone. And to top it all off, this person actually happened to be a parent of one of the students I was teaching. So it's like you're entrusting your child's development to me, and yet you don't regard me as having fully arrived?

Chapter 2

THE MYTH OF
THE ONE

"She might be the one."

When I was about nineteen years old, my best friend's mother told me that she believed her son was my husband. We were best friends. We finished each other's sentences. He was cute too! Her son, however, was gay. He was clearly very gay, but I believed his mother anyway. As odd as it sounds, we were compatible. His mother was someone who I looked up to as a woman of God and a minister, and I strongly believed that she had heard from God (as we all do in various ways). Every time I would see her, she would confirm that I was her son's wife and that someday he would be delivered, and we would be married. I would spend many days praying for him and fasting for him. I once even foolishly "sowed" an $800 "seed" into a ministry when the preacher made a call for anyone believing God to deliver one of their loved ones. I was so extreme, wanting badly for him leave his homosexual lifestyle and turn his eyes back to Jesus—and women, of course. Neither ever happened. But his mother believed it so strongly, and I wanted for her to be right. I wanted for him to be "the one." As I evolved in my thinking, I began to realize just how ridiculous it all was. We were very different people going down very different paths. Still, it was hard for me to see anyone else for years, because, after all, if God had "one" for me, and he was "the one," then how could there be any others? He wasn't the one. After awhile I stopped even wanting him to be "the one." But I wondered how any one of us could ever thwart God's plans with our own free will. After all, if he wasn't my one, did that mean she was wrong?

Unfortunately, it didn't stop there. Throughout my short lifetime, I can't tell you how many men were supposed to be my "husband," whether someone prophesied it to me or whether I conjured up the thoughts on my own.

> *To me:* "God said you're my wife."
> *To another girl:* "No, actually he said you're my wife."
> *To yet another girl:* "No, wait…I think God meant you."

Many of them are now married now, and I am still happily single. Am I to assume that all of those women are married to my husbands? Did God make a mistake? Did I make mistakes so badly that I singlehandedly ruined the will of God? Do I not hear from God at all? I know of a woman who decided one day that she was going to make a list of every quality that she wanted in a man, from his integrity to his spirituality to his physical attributes. She prayed about her list, and then the very next week, she met the man who would become her husband. He happened to have every single quality she wrote on that list. On the other hand, I have another friend who wrote a similar list: that was 15 years ago. She's still single, still praying, and still waiting. Are we to communicate a message to her that somehow she did something wrong? Is her faith lacking?

It's Just Obscure

The reason there are so many contradictions and obscurities around the concept of "the one" is that there is no such thing. Everyone's path in life is different. The way by which we establish relationships with people around us vary. The message of "the one" is complicated simply because we live in a damaged and broken world where our free will leaves us in complicated situations. People make choices, and we find ourselves tangled in a web of good and bad decisions. As a result there are many realities that we're confronted with.

Friend #1

After being married for a year and a half to her husband, he passed away due to a long battle with sickle cell anemia. They were so compatible in fact that their names rhymed. Not long after she met another wonderful man who would ask her to be his wife.

After five years, they are still married and very happy. Which one was her "one?" Her first husband, or her second husband?

Friend #2

After dating for two years, he decided to propose to his girlfriend. After a year and a half of marriage, they no longer got along and decided to call it quits. Did he give up on his "one?"

Friend #3

She married her "one" at a young age, and they stayed together for a decade until she found out her husband was cheating on her with multiple women. Their marriage failed. Did she marry the wrong "one?"

"The one" is a complicated theory mainly because human beings have free will. We can choose, think, and act within our own jurisdiction. The idea that there is one person for us suggests that one person was divinely created and set aside specifically for another person. I tend to lean toward favoring that idea; however, I cannot ignore the reality of my own free will alongside that concept. I believe they work hand in hand. I don't believe that God is so limited that our free will and choices affect God's divine appointments. Even though our free will and the broken world that we live in complicate things, I don't believe these realities avert God's plan in any way. I preached a sermon a few years ago titled "God's Only Plan A," because as human beings we feel that if one thing does not work out then the only other option is Plan B. I would argue that because God works within a divine realm, there is no such thing as Plan B with God: there is only Plan A. This, quite naturally, is a difficult concept for us to wrap our minds around. If we focus our attention on "the one," then we fail to grasp the beauty of the intricacies of God's plan. In spite of a broken world, God works tirelessly to redeem all things back to God's self, and we are major characters in that plan for redemption. Our choices and our decisions, whether we fail or succeed, are all part of that plan. It is all Plan A.

Unmerited Pressure

Placing high value on the idea that there is only one person for us leaves a great deal of room for disappointment. It's almost as though we are playing Russian roulette with life, betting on one particular number and feeling that if the wheel does not land on that number, then we will lose out. For starters, there is an unfair amount of pressure that you place on yourself. Once whoever you're seeing fails to meet those expectations or the relationship fails you, then it's easy to fall into greater despair than you would fall into after a typical breakup. This despair steals our hope, our plans, our goals, and our energy. We give our entire selves to a concept as opposed to discovering the person. Many of us even go as far as to hold onto the relationship in spite of apparent red flags for the mere fact that we are hanging onto a promise that this individual is the one. I have witnessed many people staying in damaging relationships because they were hanging onto a supposed promise. Unfortunately, I have done the same in ignoring common sense because I thought the person I was with was "the one." After several tough breakups with men who I thought were "the one" God sent me, I fell into deep depressions. Looking back I realize that part of the reason was because I would mourn the relationship, and the other part was because I felt that I had missed my one shot with the one person God had for me. In my mind there was no hope that God would send me someone else because I thought God had only one for me. I underestimated the unlimited resources of God, even in men.

"The one" theory also results in us placing unrealistic expectations on others as we seek the perfect image of this "one" character in someone else. I know people whose mentalities are clouded by their pursuit of "the one" and therefore have a hard time going out on a simple date. Their dates are then turned off because of the amount of pressure placed on them to be everything the other is hoping for. "The one" mentality does not leave room for the opportunity to evolve and grow. We want the one to fit perfectly into our idea of who they should be. We want them to fit into our world. We want someone to fit every quality on our list. And while I understand that it's important to write out and create a standard for what you feel you need in a partner, that list should be open-ended in case you meet someone whose qualities may not be on your list, but rather match who you are. I had a conversation with a young man who said to me that one woman he used to date had six out of the ten qualities he wanted in a woman. He went on to say that the woman he was currently seeing had eight out of the ten qualities that he wanted in a woman. I wondered what kind of image of perfection the woman who had ten out of the ten qualities he wanted in a woman would look like. That level of perfection doesn't exist. It causes us to seek out a mere image and shortchange the true value of someone else.

Not too long ago one of my close friends started seriously dating a man who she fell in love with. Like any good female friend, I proceeded to ask her what it was that he did in life. I wanted to know where he worked and what his talents were. I wanted to know all the qualities he had from her list. I will never forget her response. She simply said, "Nothing—he's just a good man." In that moment I realized that this man, whom she loved, didn't have to be perfect. He was just a good man who loved her and treated her with kindness and respect. He was her someone. I believe that "the one" terminology has too many loopholes and is—yet again—something else that our culture has adopted that has done more harm than good. We need to shift our language from "the one" to "someone," which is a more practical way of thinking. I believe that if it is in God's will and God has someone for us, this means that God has some person for us and that is not limited to one person, one opportunity, or one chance to get it right. You may be surprised how introducing new language can shift the mentalities of people within a particular culture. Personally, I'm not looking for "the one"—I've had plenty of those. I am looking out for someone who in the scheme of this life will choose to meet and partner with me on my journey. Then my journey will be our journey. Someone, not "the one."

Don't Kiss Dating Good-bye

In his popular book *I Kissed Dating Goodbye*, author Joshua Harris makes some great points about the importance of friendship and commitment. He suggests that dating is a broken system and a major barrier to men and women of the faith. His approach attempts to spare people from the heartache and tediousness of dating. His belief that dating should be intentional is also valid. The book suggests the developing phenomenon of courtship that many individuals and Christian ministries have adopted and applied as a teaching resource and standard for living. I believe courtship is a healthy approach to relationships. Courtship is about the intentional pursuit of another person. Within this, dating is highly discouraged. The problem with courting is that one has to date before they can even make the decision to proceed into an actual courtship. Even if you were platonic friends with an individual, once you become emotionally involved, that brings another dynamic to the relationship that can bring out something different.

A few years ago one of my closest friends and I decided that after being platonic friends for nearly a decade, we should look into pursuing a relationship with one another. The relationship had never gone beyond friendship up until that point, though we had shared many close moments over the years. We concluded that the foundation of our friendship was strong enough to pursue something more. We had a great initial conversation where we decided that because of the foundation of our friendship we would be intentional about how we would move into a courtship. Unfortunately it was not long before we realized that it was not going to work out. The two of us were completely different when it came to compatibility within the context of an emotional relationship. This was very interesting to me because within the context of our platonic friendship, we were very compatible. One of my biggest reservations was that we were having deep conversations about our future and marriage, and we hadn't even been out on two dates. Even though we had done these things before in our friendship, I just wanted to go to the movies and have dinner and hang out with him in this context before committing myself. I felt pressured to commit and overwhelmed that we weren't merely getting to know one another in this different way. We were not on the same page. I wanted to date first, and he wanted to court. I thought that our dating would lead to courtship. He thought that was wasting time. The relationship failed. What happened in our situation is not always the case when it comes to people entering into courtships. Perhaps he had courtship all wrong, and I had it right, or vice versa. Regardless, I don't believe that the courtship model should be universally applied to every situation.

In her online blog called "Love, Joy, Feminism," author Libby Anne writes this response to Harris's *I Kissed Dating Goodbye*:

> Joshua Harris taught me that dating was wrong. He taught
> me that having relationships that didn't lead to marriage
> was wrong. As a result, my first romantic relationship was
> serious from day one. It was all about "is this the person
> I'm going to marry or not?" I obsessed over that question.
> I knew that if I broke up with him I would be damaged
> goods, but also that I should break up with him immedi-
> ately if I felt our relationship was not leading to marriage.
> I regret this.[xi]

Dating is an essential part to relationships; therefore, I don't suggest kissing it good-bye. The dating system is not broken; people are. It doesn't matter how great a system is, if the people are internally broken, the relationship will fail, and that includes courtship. Furthermore we should not look at every single person we come across asking ourselves if they are our husband or wife. Naturally, many people do this because of human curiosity, but to implement a system of spouse hunting as opposed to guiding people into making wise choices can be risky. All relationships will not lead to marriage. Some dates will not make it past one night of dinner. And that's OK. They are not all supposed to. We are all taking in information and evolving from it. At the same time, this does not mean that we should be frivolous in our dat-ing either. If people decide they want to implement the courtship model into their relationships, then that is their decision. As well, one should not look down on those who decide to date. Many within the Christian community have manipulated people into thinking that common dating is wrong. On the contrary, it can be a very healthy thing.

Life is about making choices, and that also includes our relationships. There is no way of escaping the reality of heartache in those choices. Human suffering is an inevitable part of our existence just as much as joy and celebration are. This is the paradox of the human experience. In Christian theology suffering is a necessary part of redemption. Suffering comes in many different forms and layers and includes (but is not exclusive to) relational suffering. In that, we have a great responsibility to make decisions that are best for our self-preservation. Sometimes those decisions don't turn out in our favor, but the good news is that we can glean from those experiences in hopes to grow personally, and for some, apply those to other relationships.

It Lies in the Decision

There is power in making choices but there is also great risk. I believe many people lean on "the one" theory to avoid the responsibility of choice. One of the major risks is the possibility of making the wrong choice. Another one for many Christians is that if their choice doesn't fit an image acceptable to our faith community, then they fear being criticized. It can be much simpler relinquishing all of the responsibility of mate choosing to God. Lastly, making choices can be a tedious thing. You have to analyze, evaluate, and invest time and energy into deciding if something is a right fit for you. There are endless directions our choices can go in. Another risk is that after that evaluating, the other person has to be on the same page as you. There is a good chance they may not be, which is why good communication is so important to any relationship. We cannot afford to cast off our power of choice because we are afraid of the risks. Furthermore, we cannot hesitate for fear that our choices hinder God's will. We have free will just as much as God has an ultimate plan for our lives.

Take for example, Hannah, a blogger from Washington, DC. She recently wrote what turned into a very popular blog post, called "My Husband Is Not My Soul Mate.[xii]" On her one-year anniversary, she decided to publicly announce her rejection of soul mates. This post was rather ironic, given her self-confessed undying love for her husband.

> Do you remember those awesome Evangelical '90s/early 2000s where Jesus was kind of like our boyfriend, and we all kissed dating good-bye because we just knew that God was going to bring us THE ONE and then life would be awesome? And THE ONE would most likely be a worship minister, or at the very least a youth pastor, and we would have to be in college when we would meet at some sort of rally to save children from disease or something....We would get married, and it would be awesome FOREVER.

Growing up, Hannah's dreams of God's plan for "the one" were shattered when her "theologian biblical scholar father" shared with her the incongruities of the soul mate theory.

> And then he gave me some of the best relationship advice I ever got: There is no biblical basis to indicate that God has one soul mate for you to find and marry. You could have a great marriage with any number of compatible people. There is no ONE PERSON for you. But once you marry someone, that person becomes your one person.

She came to realize that her choices were enriched with God's provision. When she met and fell in love with her husband, he chose to love her, as she did him. She stated that her love for him was in her decision to love him. She says that her delight is in choosing to love her husband every day. Ultimately it all comes down to the decision you make to love someone. Of course there need to be factors that draw you in to allow you to make that decision like character, attraction, history, values, and so forth. But overall, you decide who to love. God will guide us, but God will not force us. Everyone that I know who is married made the decision to get married. The person they decided to marry fit with who they were, though that person may not necessarily have been any more or less flawed than any other person they may have dated in life. They just as easily could have chosen to marry any of them as well. There is a great deal of power in decision making. We see it from the very beginning of scripture in the book of Genesis when the man and the woman that God created had a decision to make. Even though that decision was unwise and ultimately led to some tragic consequences, God did not intervene in their decision making. God allowed them to carry through with their created right. And God will allow us to do the same.

SINCERELY, SINGLE & NOT LOOKING

"" I remember-I must have been in my midtwenties out of college-I was going to church and trying to get connected to the people. I had been going for several months, and they had a women's retreat out in the mountains. I thought this would be a fantastic opportunity to connect. They had different workshops, and I went to one of them. I started to notice some of the language on how to be a better woman or how to be a better wife. I sat through them, and they talked about these subjects, and I thought it was odd and not what I expected. By the end of the workshops, they would say "Raise your hands, those of you who are single, and we're going to pray for you to get a spouse." Again, I thought it was so weird. It really bothered me that this would be something that would happen at this retreat. It wasn't what I expected. It just couldn't be women talking about other things. It was a major disappointment. It opened my eyes in how the church viewed women, especially single women. If you're single, you need to get married and you need to have kids and your place is in the home. We don't care if you have degrees or if you're educated, you're supposed to be in the home.

I did go to one church later on that had a singles group, and even though it was a group of divorced people, I thought it was pretty cool. We did things together a lot, but what started to happen is they started getting married, and I realized that it wasn't about connecting with others—it was about looking for a mate, which was also disappointing because I was looking to make friends. I remember this one time these two new guys from another church came to one of our meetings, and we were putting together a game night. They said they would bring their friends from their singles ministry. So when game night came around, they came and brought all their friends, and it wound up being a complete meat market. It was like their singles ministry coming to jump on our singles ministry. I was thinking, "Wait—I thought we were just going to hang out?" This was just so odd to me. It was never my pastor's intention for it to be that way. He just knew we needed a place to connect with community.

I remember in college my married friends saying, "We can't wait for the man God has for you." I remember thinking that I didn't believe there was a "one." That was not anything I was praying for then. I was just living my life and trying to be the person God wanted me to be. I noticed that Bible colleges would tend to try to get students together. They were like eighteen and nineteen years old. I feel like in our culture there's definitely a message that singles are second-class citizens. Like there's the idea that there's something more for them, and the church tries to groom them in that direction whether they want to be or not. It's like "Don't you want to get married? Don't you want to have kids?" The message is to come along and be like the rest of us. There's an expectation of purity-not that there is anything wrong with that-but I know friends personally who met in the church and two months into the relationship, they were like "We have to get married because we want to have sex, and we just can't wait." I said to them, "What— you're going to get married, and it's only been two months?" They didn't even know each other a year, and they were getting married. How is this healthy and productive and loving?

Chapter 3

THE MYTH OF
THE VIRGIN MARY

*"Whatever you do, don't have
sex or have any babies out of wedlock."*

My introduction to sexuality came when I was young. I honestly don't remember the age, but I think it could have been somewhere around five or six. When my brother and I were younger, our parents would take us to Rocky Mount, North Carolina, for the summer to spend time with our cousins. Our grandmother and great-aunt would take care of us. We made friends easily with the kids in the neighborhood, and we would play all day in the streets and park until the streetlights came on. One day I went with one of my friends, my cousin, and her mother to visit some of their family, not too far away. My memory is very vague, but it was one of those country houses with lots of land and a long driveway to get to the house. When we pulled up and went inside, the woman's mother asked me to lock the screen door behind them while they went into the kitchen. For some reason I was having a hard time with the lock, so my friend's uncle came to help me. He locked the door, but he did something else. He slipped his hand down my pants and began touching my private parts. I was confused, so I pulled away. I went to make sure the door was secure, and once again, he put his hands down my pants. I finally told him to stop and moved away, walking quickly into the kitchen where my friend's mother was sitting and sat by her the entire time we were there. He would walk into the kitchen where we sat a few times, giving a sly smile, and I would look away. My friend's mother kept asking me what was wrong, but I wouldn't say.

When we finally left the house, I sat in the back seat and ducked my head below as though I was hiding. For the rest of the evening, I "hid," so to speak. I didn't say much, and I spent a lot of time sitting near family members. I didn't want to be alone, but every time someone would ask me what was wrong, I would not say. Though my memory, as I said earlier, is vague, I can understand the confusion children who are ever placed in a situation like that feel. They don't know what sexuality even is but have an intuitive knowledge of its perversion. Because of this, they are feeling one thing but cannot articulate it. I do not claim to know the feelings of every single child in these types of situations, but I do know what I felt as a six-year-old. The most interesting thing to me about this experience is that I barely remember it and have no idea how it may or may not have affected me. Personally, I can see manifestations of how other things affected me as I grew up, but since I was so young and clueless as to what was happening, and because it happened so quickly, I can't say. Other people can tell stories of early abuse and be able to tie it to something in particular, but I honestly cannot. What I can say, however, is that this was my introduction into the world of sexuality.

In 1994 I went to a conference called DC '94, a Christian conference designed to help students see their identity in Christ. I remember being particularly excited about this conference because it was only for teenagers, and even though I was only twelve years old, I was in a higher grade and allowed to attend. It was like any other church trip could be expected to be, with a bunch of hormonal teenagers spending an entire week in a hotel with only the sporadic guidance of a few chaperones. I never fit in. I was always the youngest girl. I was always the most socially awkward, not having discovered at that time how to navigate my introverted nature. My inability to socialize worked to my advantage though, because it caused me to pay attention more in general sessions and workshops. I was enamored by how grandiose everything was. There were thousands of junior-high and high-school students, all gathered in the large DC convention center. The music was loud, and the guest speakers were all engaging.

On the last day of the conference, the speaker for the general session spoke on purity and committing our bodies to the Lord. At the end of his sermon, he had the ushers pass out small cards to every single student in the room. The top of the card read "Commitment Card." It was for each of us to sign and commit to remaining virgins until we were married. I took this pledge very seriously. I knew that by signing that card and turning it in, God was watching me. I was only twelve years old, but I understood that promises weren't meant to be broken.

I believe that this commitment I made in my heart and on that postcard was the reason I was a late bloomer when it came to anything even remotely sexual. My older cousin, who lived with us when I was in middle school, would have pornographic videotapes or magazines lying around, but I never felt compelled to engage or act on any feelings. To be honest, I don't remember having any intense hormonal feelings until late in high school. Most girls in high school had had their first kiss when they were in the seventh grade. I was embarrassed that by my junior year, I hadn't had my first real kiss. When I finally did, it was because I felt obligated to. I wanted to get it over with so I could see what the big deal was about. All the while the message I kept receiving in church was to wait. The key word that I consistently heard was abstinence. Sure, maybe we'd have the occasional speaker come by to talk to the youth about sex, but for the most part, it was the same message. I dared not have any conversations with my parents, I was too embarrassed, though now I realize it was necessary.

Through college I dated here and there and "made out" with a few boys but nothing anywhere near close to sex. I had made a commitment to God to remain a virgin until marriage, and I was determined to stick to that. But my decision was more than that card I signed in 1994. I heard countless sermons and messages about the importance of abstinence as a Christian. I thought I would go to hell if I had sex. I thought that perhaps I'd be damaged goods of some sort. I thought that I would disappoint God, which was the worst of them all. As I grew in my faith, this commitment became more important to me, and into my early twenties, I still wasn't dating much. In the back of my mind, I was waiting for "the one." I thought that once "the one" came, then first would come love, then marriage, then sex, then the baby in the baby carriage. It didn't quite happen that way.

Once I got into seminary, I went on a dating binge. I think it's because I thought that every man there was a man of God, which should automatically mean that they were good men in general. I learned the hard way—in and out of seminary—that a supposed man of God is still a man. I studied hard in seminary, but I also dated hard. That's when I began to explore my sexuality a bit more, ironically. My seminary had a great academic reputation, but I also heard of a subculture within it where students explored their sexuality, both hetero and homo. I would hear countless stories of sexual orgies, hook-ups, and students (mostly men) traveling to preachers' conferences and cheating on their girlfriends and spouses in the worst kind of ways. I vowed to stay away from all of it, yet somehow found myself intrigued. There was a thin line between spirituality and sexuality in this incubus of spiritual leaders—two concepts that had remained separate my entire life. I was curious.

My studies and new ways of thinking slowly changed my views on Christianity, faith, and ministry, which also included me questioning why I was waiting to have sex. By now I was about twenty-four years old. During all of this, I was dating different men, and I adopted the philosophy that so many who claim to be celibate adopt: it's called the "everything but" philosophy. I thought that if I did "everything but" have sex, then I really wasn't having sex. I know people personally whose entire preaching platform is based on the fact that they didn't have sex until they were married, when the reality is they just didn't have physical intercourse, but they fail to mention the fact that they did everything else. To me, oral sex, hand jobs, and anything involving an orgasm equates to a sexual experience. Those of us who have engaged in all of that up until the moment of saying "I do" and who then testify that we waited are only fooling ourselves. I was not having actual intercourse but was engaging in sexual activity. I felt like I was safe. That didn't last long.

My last year I got close with a man I called my friend. I saw him then as a man I loved, but I know now I never did. I was attracted to his pain and made it my mission to be its remedy. I loved who I wanted him to be and tried to make him to be, but never was. When we met he was fresh out of an engagement, and everyone (I mean everyone) warned the both of us not to enter into anything too intense too hastily. Unfortunately that describes exactly what the relationship was: too intense and too hasty. His role as an up-and-coming pastor and his kind heart kept me pushing forward. I remember the first time I had the courage to tell him that I felt we shouldn't continue because of how fast we were going. I didn't think he was ready (and now, looking back, neither was I). That was the day he told me he loved me. It was only two months into the relationship and three months past his engagement. I knew he didn't really love me. I knew that he truly believed that he did at the time, but because of his fragile emotional state, he was attached to me in a very unreal way. I didn't care. For a while, we were growing as friends, spending lots of time together, studying and doing things seminary students do. I thought we were building on something when in actuality we were both just digging a hole. My issues with men and trust would surface in ways that were uncomfortable for him. His issues with commitment and relationships would surface in ways that would betray me. As a result, things just got worse. As they got worse, the friendship got diminished as the months went on. We continued spending many nights together "not" having sex but almost having sex, and that became the nature of our relationship, because we didn't have a relationship. There was no commitment, no titles. I think he knew that he shouldn't have entered into anything with anyone as quickly as we did, so he would be careful not to publicly display our relationship to his friends or family. That hurt me, but I sucked it up. The communication died off, yet my unhealthy attachment grew more and more. After graduating from seminary, I would see him less and less. He would text periodically, but I had no understanding of what the nature of our relationship was. There were no discussions and nothing to offer me the closure that I now realize I needed. Unfortunately those signs and countless other red flags were not enough for me to back away. We saw each other three times that summer, and the last time we saw each other was the time I would lose my virginity to him. I was twenty-six years old.

I can't say I didn't know it was going to happen. I went to his place to visit him for the first time since he'd moved. I remember walking through his apartment looking at all of the pictures of his family and friends and being faced with the reality that I wasn't included in any of them. I didn't feel a part of his life and I didn't feel welcome, but there was a part of me that wanted to force my way in as I had tried and failed so many times before. Our decision to have sex that day was my way of forcing myself in. It was my way of thinking that this act would keep us connected. It was a very warped way of thinking that you wouldn't expect from someone who'd waited twenty-six years to have sex. I didn't feel any regrets. I assumed that this act had somehow defined our relationship without words. We left later to head to a restaurant to have dinner, and I remember trying to grab his hand and him letting go immediately. This was the single most significant display of how he truly felt about me at the time. I don't think it was intentional. I believe that this was a man who was conflicted and damaged, and I got caught in the crossfire. I thought to myself, "We just had sex, and he won't even hold my hand in public?" It couldn't be. I couldn't have just given this man a gift that I had not given to anyone in my entire life, and he still wouldn't acknowledge a connection. That's because there was no connection, and I was in denial.

I didn't hear from him much after that day. He would tell me he was going out of town, and I would receive a text message or two from him periodically that would send me in a downward spiral. Nothing changed. I gave him my mind, my emotions, and finally my body, and I received nothing in return. I sent him an e-mail explaining how I felt, and after nothing changed I sent him an infamous "it's over" text. We didn't speak after that for a month. I would cry every day for hours upon hours. No one would have ever known what I was going through because I didn't want anyone to know how I had failed so miserably. I was the girl who had sex with the guy for the first time, and he in essence didn't call me back. I thought I had an image to uphold, so when people worried and asked, I would just say that I was "going through" something. I would share with no one except a handful of close friends I felt comfortable sharing it with because they were in similar places in life. I wish I could say that the story ended there, but it didn't. After weeks of not speaking, I finally tracked him down, and he agreed to meet to talk. That talk turned into a few years of speaking and then not speaking for months and then speaking again. It would turn into more lack of commitment and obscure boundaries. It would turn into other sexual experiences, because I thought that was the only way of keeping his attention. My attraction and interest in him grew less and less, but that didn't matter because for some reason I thought if we were together, then all I had invested wouldn't be in vain. I wanted so badly for this man to commit to me, but the reality was, he could not. He would tell me, "I cannot commit to you, Khristi," and to this day I do not blame him for how he was feeling. I did however blame him for how he handled it early on. Here's the thing, ladies and gentlemen: if someone tells you that he or she cannot commit to you, walk away. You cannot force a man or a woman to commit to you just as much as you cannot force them to love you. I know it's painful to hear those words and to face those realities, but I guarantee you, the pain will be even greater the longer you continue to push and stay in denial. You want to be able to love yourself enough to walk away. You want to be able to have enough hope for the future to leave room for someone who would lay down his or her life for you.

At that point, I was no longer the image of the virgin waiting until she got married—poised, stable, and mature. I was no longer that confident twelve-year-old who signed that commitment card all those years ago. I was emotionally out of control, miserable, and harmfully attached. Through unfortunate circumstances, God had to make me release that person because on my own I was not willing. It was costing me too much. When I did decide to experience sex with another man, it was because I thought that somehow my encounter with him would erase the tragedy of my first experiences. It didn't. It only made it worse. It's unfortunate that I had to experience sex this way. There are moments when

I think to myself, "Had I known better I would have done it differently." Well, I didn't know better, and I blame no one for that. These experiences were necessary in shaping me into the person that I am today. Still, I can't help but wonder if those vague messages regarding sex that I had received my entire life had anything to do with my choices. I did not have a holistic sexual ethic. I just knew that sex was something you shouldn't do if you weren't married. After a while, that alone, was not enough.

SEXUAL MISEDUCATION

I often wonder about the young woman who is told all her life that she should wait to have sex until she gets married. Furthermore, every time sex is even brought up, it is hushed or swept under the carpet. The topic of sex is taboo, and many times the message that's communicated to Christians is one that is negative in nature. Often, sex is equated to being something that is bad. I wonder what happens when that young woman does wait until she is married and is finally on her wedding night. How is she supposed to make that mental transition? Is that transition expected to be smooth? A young woman, who for twenty-five or thirty years of her life, has been communicated a negative message about sex and is supposed to turn into a sexual deviant in one night. There is an unrealistic approach and lack of proper sexual education within the Christian community.

Historically the phrase "out of wedlock" was used to describe someone who had sex and/or conceives a child outside of the context of marriage. "Out of wedlock" is something you don't want to be. I always associated that phrase with hellfire and brimstone because it was used so often that it was a position I was literally afraid to ever find myself in. While it continues to be used in some spaces, as time has progressed, many people have moved out of that expression. I believe this is mainly because statistics reflect a rise in the number of people engaging in sexual activity and having children outside of marriage.

Christian culture has historically imposed a puritanical narrative of sexuality that suggests that sex is exceedingly sinful outside of marriage. As a result, real conversations about sex are left explicitly for those who are married. The times that sex is mentioned is when those married remind those who are single of what they "have in store" for them when they do get married. Other times are when those who are single are reminded, time and time again, to wait. In a recent conversation, my friend Jacob Heiss, an associate pastor, described to me his perspective of our culture's incomplete sexual ethic. He said:

> We have not worked out a sexual ethic that works pragmatically for the people who are to believe it. So why should we expect people who don't believe it to get on board? It's a ridiculous expectation. Because we have not done the hard work of hammering out our own sexual ethic, we have been unable to communicate the shape that the gospel takes with respect to the sexual part of our

lives. You see it even with respect to the married/single dynamic. We treat single people as if they're nonsexual beings, yet with the propensity for error. So sexuality is just something we're supposed to harness and keep at bay until you achieve that married state of affairs at which point you can release it. But we don't tell people how to express themselves in a healthy sexual way, except for in negative terms.

I was on a retreat a few years ago with peers, and as we watched a movie, a scene sexual in nature came on. The young man next to me put his hands over his eyes and said, "Let me know when it's over." I understand that because his commitment to live a life-style of abstinence, it was important for him to stay away from sexual images planted in his mind. In spite of my understanding, the image of him covering his eyes reflects how I believe our community wants single people to respond to sex: to cover our eyes and pretend it's not there. No sexual ethic or even guideline. Just don't do it.

The Christian community has also unintentionally elevated the image of a preteenage virgin, whose standard many women (and some men) are encouraged to live up to. This is the image of the iconic Virgin Mary, mother of Jesus. I tend to believe a great deal of emphasis scripturally was placed on Mary's virginity to highlight the miracle of Christ's birth. It is impossible for a virgin to give birth; therefore, the evidence of Jesus's divinity is undeniable. However, the church has placed considerable weight on the virginity of Mary in relation to her sexuality and in turn placed those standards on others. I'm not saying that this is not a standard one should strive to live up to, but rather the complexities that come with it are too dense.

When it comes to sex, the Christian community is drowning in ambiguities, and I believe that this conservative neglect has backfired and in turn created hypersexual tension. Christians are arguably a sexually repressed, sexually uneducated, and sexually careless group of people, given the sexual moral high ground that we stand on. In the book *Half the Sky*, which thoroughly gives account of women's oppression worldwide, authors Nicholas D. Kristoff and Sheryl WuDunn describe the countries "with the most straight-laced and sexually conservative societies" as being the ones with the largest issues of prostitution.[xiii] I make this correlation because the irony of the "morally superior" is that they often live out the antithesis of their platform. We've seen it in preachers "falling from grace;" we've seen it in church scandals, deacons excommunicated from church, and mistresses confessing during testimony service. Similarly we've seen it in the political sphere, in which politicians often pride themselves on public heterosexual marriages. Again, I'm not saying that there's anything wrong with holding to a sturdy position on how one should live out his or her sexuality. That position, however, should be well informed, honest, faith-driven, and held alongside realistic systems of accountability. Here is what Rodney Clapp concludes in *Families at the Crossroads*:

> Virginity is no great and saintly virtue in and of itself. Sexual activity is not inherently corrupting, but we should also avoid what could be called the "new-fangled" misinterpretation of the text. Immoderate misinterpretation correctly sees that there's nothing sinful about sex and that it is indeed a great good and can be enjoyed. But the modern misinterpretation incorrectly proceeds to imagine that the most important thing a celibate person gives up is sex. Ironically both the old-fashioned and the newfangled views are sex-obsessed. The old-fashioned is obsessed with sex because it sees sex as uniquely corrupted. The new-fangled is obsessed with sex because it sees sex as utterly necessary to any full and happy life.[xiv]

Its Power. Its Purpose.

Even though our culture would say otherwise, sex is much more than a leisure activity. We have turned sex into a hobby likened to playing a basketball game or going out and taking a light jog. Our innate sexual impulses have led us to naturally conclude that it is a frivolous act.

"I want to get laid, so I'm gonna go get laid."

This is oftentimes a more natural tendency for men because sex is more physical for men, while women may understand the "sex is powerful" concept because it is more emotionally tied for us. The best example I can think of is this: even though you could pick up a gun and go shoot someone, because you understand the power and implications of those actions, you don't do so easily. This is in spite of the fact that you have all the freedom in the world to do so. By human nature we are self-preserving people, so if we feel threatened, we could quite naturally pick up a gun and use it on another person. Of course sex is not to be equated to killing someone, but my point is that freedom and impulse do not automatically equate to permission. My friend Kim Copeland described her perception of the power of sex to me this way:

> I didn't have the language to talk about sex until I started practicing yoga, because one of the lenses of yoga is called *Brahmacharya*. In Sanskrit it means "be chased." It means be chased not for the traditional reasons, like sex is bad, but it literally means that it's powerful. Everyone who's ever had sex can say that it's a powerful experience. *Ahmisa* means cause "no harm," which is also a tenant of yoga. You hold the two together and you say, I know that this is a powerful thing because I can be a part of something that could potentially be harmful to someone. I really need to explore all the ways that it could potentially produce harm before I enter into it. Having sex with someone I'm not serious about could potentially harm me or that other person because it's not just about harming

you—it's about harming the other person. You having sex casually might not harm you, but it can harm the other person.

This way of thinking would and should make all of us more careful about whom we enter into sexual relationships with. Because of the powerful exchange that comes with it, it's best to engage within the context of a lifelong, committed, mutual, monogamous relationship. I believe that it takes time to establish that kind of love.

This is a philosophy that is at the foundation of how I guide men and women. However, there is much more to it than that. Healthy and honest conversations about intercourse, hormones, masturbation, STDs, the increasing accessibility of pornography, orgasmic experience, and many other aspects of sexuality are necessary conversations that need to take place in the church, in the home, and in the classroom. Looking back, I didn't even know that a part of the sexual experience is having an actual orgasm. I didn't realize that I wasn't having a pleasurable sexual experience when I did have sex because I was never taught that one should include it. I feel bad that I haven't had these conversations with my younger sister. I have to admit that I, too, have fallen into that cyclical trap of wanting to project a message to her that it's better to just ignore it altogether until her wedding night—then we can talk about it. Not only is that way of thinking harmful, but it is unrealistic in the hypersexualized culture that she is very much a part of, already receiving these messages on a daily basis.

I once heard the story of a young woman who waited until she was married to have her first sexual experience. After two weeks of marriage, she decided to confide in a friend and complained about how much she hated sex. Outside of the fact that I'm sure it may have hurt or been uncomfortable for her first time, I wondered how much of that had to do with the messages she received about sex before she was married. It is possible that she could have merely been having bad sexual experiences. It's also possible that the lack of education she received about sex early on may have contributed to her experience. There are so many married women who do not have a healthy sexuality because they were taught all their lives that sex is bad. Then, when it comes time for sex to be used in the context of a marriage, they are not only clueless, but they have developed a "sex is bad" perspective. All of a sudden, they are expected to shift. That Virgin Mary image continues even in the bedroom. In many cases it either backfires, and young girls have an unhealthy curiosity about sex and experiment in ways that are damaging, or you have those who wait until they're married but on their honeymoon night are unable to change the perspective that has been deeply entrenched in their psyche that sex is a bad thing. There are many layers to the lack of adequate teaching in the Christian community when it comes to sex that I cannot properly cover all of the effects it's had.

EFFEMINATE PURITY

I once saw a message on Twitter that said, "Jesus will return for a pure and spotless bride...not a soiled and somewhat dirty one." The bride that this person was referring to is a metaphoric one in the bride of the church to Christ, and he is no doubt suggesting that the church pursue righteousness instead of coveting the things of the world. Even though this man meant well, this tweet made me cringe. The language was so strong and reflected words that have been traditionally used in Christian culture that I believe have done more harm than good. We have consistently suggested that perfection is unattainable apart from Christ. We've used phrases like "we are sinners saved by grace." But the purity teaching incorporates language that would suggest otherwise. Dictionary.com defines purity as follows:

pu·ri·ty [pyoor-i-tee] noun

1. The condition or quality of being pure; freedom from anything that debases, contaminates, pollutes, etc.: the purity of drinking water.
2. Freedom from any admixture or modifying addition.
3. Ceremonial or ritual cleanness.
4. Freedom from guilt or evil; innocence.
5. Physical chastity; virginity.[xv]

The problem with purity is humanity. Our innate human nature contradicts the idea that we can reach inherent cleanness, even though the Christian community adheres to the idea that this cleanness can be obtained only through Christ. Still there is pressure to live a life of purity. Though living a life of purity can be associated with many areas, we place a great deal of emphasis on purity as it relates to sex. To be pure means to live a life of chastity. This can be problematic when people either "slip up" or choose to have sex. The message that is sent to them is that they are impure. Having the idea in your mind that you are somehow dirty can lead to serious insecurities. No one wants to be dirty. I had a close friend who was engaged and decided to abstain from sex in her relationship with her fiancé. This was public knowledge to the people around her. We were proud that they followed through with that level of discipline. One day, after I had shared with her my story about my early sexual experiences and the lessons I learned, she confessed to me early stories of sexual experimentation. I could tell that she opened up to me because I had shared my story. I could also sense that she was very insecure about that part of her story and chose not to share with others for fear they would look at her differently. This was unfortunate because she was such a wise and gifted woman who I felt had a great deal to offer in her entire story.

I spoke with an African woman who perceives the purity message to be a distinctive message within American culture with a particular emphasis on girls:

Purity rings are a very American thing. If you go to certain parts of Africa or some parts of even Europe, the concept of the purity ring is very much a thing of American Christian culture. It points to that idea that you're waiting for that one, especially for women. I feel like the pressure is more on them. It's almost like Christian women in America hold this responsibility more than guys do. Who gets the ring? It's the girl.

I understood her perspective, though it's clear in many other countries that virginity is an expectation of girls and women. That expectation persists in American Christian culture. I very rarely hear purity messages associated with boys or men. We have made the term effeminate. Purity ministries in churches are typically focused on targeting girls ages thirteen to eighteen. Purity conferences are also targeted toward young girls. The conferences display images of teenage girls dressed in white gowns wearing princess tiaras, dancing with their fathers as they remind them of their value. Girls are taught at a young age to preserve themselves, while boys are unintentionally encouraged to explore or are given the excuse that because they are boys, then naturally things will happen. I had a male friend tell me that his sister had a "rite of passage" ceremony when she was younger, all centered on purity. His sister waited to have sex until she got married. He said that while his sister had been given the purity message, he always felt that he somehow had had a pass because it wasn't insisted upon for him. He did not wait to have sex until he was married because he never felt he had to. In a separate conversation, another male friend said something similar in his assessment of the gender gap with the purity message:

> Part of it is a practical matter. You're not going to invest time, energy, and effort trying to convince boys to abstain until they're married because it's rare to find a male who is interested in waiting. Experience would say that men are less likely to wait until they're married to have sex. Most people aren't going to put their energy in investing in boys to abstain until they're married. It's like playing the odds.

He went on to say:

> I've personally had men in leadership positions in the church say things like "enjoy yourself while you're young" and "get yours" in reference to sleeping with multiple women. I got a little nod and a wink as if to say "go ahead and go through with it but don't beat yourself up if you want it." But with young girls there is no wink and nod. There is no "give it your best shot." It's "this is what is expected of you." Women are encouraged to abstain. Men are encouraged to "try really hard." This creates a great deal of tension among women and men. Women are

trying as hard as they can not to give in, while men are trying hard to get you to give in. We need the same message,
a universal one, in order to avoid these contradictions.

I agree with him wholeheartedly in that if we are going to
send a message, it needs to be a universal one. Purity is contradictory in both human nature and gender. While the foundation of
the message is useful, it lacks cohesiveness.

ESTABLISHING A SEXUAL ETHIC

It's important to understand why you are deciding to live out
your sexuality in a particular way, and then it's equally important
for you to commit to that decision. Gone are the days when it is
enough to just simply state that you are waiting and believe that
will be enough to sustain you in the long run. We need to evolve in
our thought, language, and behavior. As you move toward prayer
and evaluating the various spheres of sexuality, your thinking will
begin to expand. A change in language should follow, moving
away from phrases like "I'm saving myself for marriage," which has
come to mean that if you do have sex before, then you have committed sexual suicide. The gospel of grace leaves room for growth,
not necessarily for excuses. I have encouraged women and men to
say things like, "I am committing my sexuality to God" or "I am
recommitting my sexuality." These types of phrases move beyond
words like "saving" or "preserving" as though you are keeping
bread from spoiling. Your body is a powerful tool. Therefore you

have to own it as such, even down to how you speak about how you govern it. Evolving thought and evolving language will then work alongside evolving behavior. This is all a part of establishing a durable sexual ethic.

After reading the book *Half the Sky,* I realized that so many women (and men) all over the world do not get to make choices about their bodies. There are women and young girls being forced into sexual violence and prostitution every minute of every day, while others become sex workers because it is a means of earning income for their families. I thought to myself, "I am living in a context where I have freedom of choice over my own body; how dare I treat that lightly? How dare I not have a healthy, developed, sexual ethic as a means of governing my body?" I have the opportunity to make a thought-out decision that many millions of women worldwide don't get the opportunity to do. It's not enough to tell some young girl or boy that her or his body is the temple of the Holy Spirit (1 Corinthians 6:19-20). They need to be educated on what that means and encouraged to think things through after they have been well informed. The philosophy you adhere to will inform your practice.

To help guide you in thought, ask yourself some of the following questions:

1) **Do you view sex as good or bad?**

2) What messages have you received about sex from your family? Your church (if it applies)? Pop culture? School?

3) Are you a virgin? If so, is there a reason why?

4) Have you had one or several sexual experiences? What was your thought process behind those decisions?

Only respond to these questions if your sexual experiences were voluntary. If involuntary in any way, please move on to the next question, and I encourage you to work out your sexual development with a counselor

5) Why do you believe God created sex?

6) How have you decided to govern your body when it comes to sex? How has this affected you?

SINCERELY,
BROKEN PAST

❝ My mom told me at a young age that sex was supposed to be between a husband and wife. But from when I was a young girl, I was physically abused by her and sexually by my dad and other people. I was really little-probably like kindergarten. My parents got a divorce early on and they had joint custody, so my brother and I would stay at my dad's house on the weekends from about kindergarten to fifth grade. I remember not feeling comfortable around him and always feeling dirty. We would stay with him and fall asleep in his room, and I'd fall asleep with my brother but would always wake up next to my dad, which would confuse me. I know now that I was being sexually abused on these and other occasions. I don't know how long this happened because in a way I blocked it out. Growing up I felt like a sexual magnet for my dad and other men. The last time I was sexually abused was when I was in the fifth grade. From that point on, I had really low self-confidence, and it was hard for me to trust people and make friends. My whole image of what love should have been was broken and shattered. I always felt I had to carry a certain image.

I was really unhappy.

I didn't understand what it meant to be in a relationship. In middle school I started messing around with guys and hooking up here and there. I thought "do whatever and have fun." I started sleeping with guys in the eighth grade. I willingly lost my virginity when I was fourteen. Again, I didn't understand how sacred God considered the physical aspect of a relationship. After I turned fifteen, my mom wanted me to go into rehab because I kept acting out and getting in trouble. I told her she was crazy because it wasn't like I was a prostitute. Around that time I accepted a relationship with Christ after years of resisting it.

After that my first boyfriend was a part of my church. We dated for two years, and I struggled in it. It wasn't so much with loving God, but with loving God over the relationship. We started having sex right away. It's not like we did it often, but we did spend a lot of time together. When I was with him, I felt like trash, but it didn't have to do with my faith. It never felt good or satisfying. I never felt like we were connecting. I just felt like a body that was being used, and I don't know if that's because of my past or that's the way the relationship was, but it never felt right. After I broke up with him, I realized how much I had compromised. It was overall a bad relationship.

I promised God after that I wouldn't have sex with another person who wasn't my husband. I don't care how close I might be to a person; I wouldn't give myself up to anyone. In giving myself up that way, it hurt me so much. I wanted to hold on to a piece of myself and be in control and when it's the right time, it's the right time. I feel like sex is created for marriage. My fiancé now is a virgin, and in the beginning of our relationship, I was afraid. I thought, "Who is going to accept me with my past?" Now I know what love is, and it's not just about the physical—that's just the bonus.

Chapter 4

THE MYTH OF
THE PERFECT IMAGE

"I've got to carry myself the way a woman of God should."

In spite of a stable upbringing, I didn't have a healthy perception of relationships growing up, nor did I have any idea how to navigate one. I grew up in a loving family, but we had our fair share of issues. My parents were evolving in their own lives, managing their intense, full-time working schedules, two kids (and later a third), and maneuvering through the complexities of their own relationship. I was a temperamental teenager and struggled with identity issues. I had a bad case of the "too's." I felt I was too fat, too dark, too unattractive, too dumb, and too untalented. Early instances of emotional trauma coupled with all of those other growing pains infused within me a false and psychologically harmful sense of self. That was the basis for how I would function in future relationships. The sad part is that I had no idea. Most people living in dysfunction, or with a dysfunctional mentality, don't realize it right away. It typically takes something to expose it.

Throughout middle school, junior high, and high school, I struggled with my identity, particularly when it came to relationships with the opposite sex. For a good part of my adolescence, I attended predominately white suburban schools. That is an interesting position for any young black girl to be in as she seeks to define who she is in relation to the people around her. As a result of this, as young, hormonal boys and girls are attempting to develop relationships with one another, I was always left out. I remember one instance in the seventh grade when I went to a friend's birthday party; we played the infamous "spin the bottle" game. I remember being particularly uncomfortable playing this game, not because I didn't want to kiss any boys, but because I wondered to myself, "Who would want to kiss me—the only black girl in the group?" I remember when the bottle landed on me. I could see the look of disappointment on the boy's face when he realized that he had to kiss me. I tried to give him an out and tell him that he didn't have to, but everyone pressured him because those were the rules of the game. When I grew a little older, my schools began to be more diverse. It went from me feeling like the oddball out because I was the only black girl to me feeling insecure because, out of the few black girls there, I was the darkest one. Most of the young black boys did not want a dark girl. It wasn't until I transferred to a very diverse private high school that any boys started paying me attention.

I didn't date much in high school. I talked to the occasional basketball player by default because I was a basketball player and spent a great deal of time with my school's teams. Again, I was a late bloomer when it came to men and relationships. I was just getting my first kiss at sixteen years old, far from understanding how to navigate within the context of a real relationship. In college I dated a young man for about six or seven months my freshman year, and that was around the time two significant things began to surface in my life. Number one, I began to grow stronger in my faith and decided sometime during the course of my freshman year that I was going to commit to the faith that had been instilled in me as a young girl. I like to look at it as though I began to mature in my faith. The second thing that occurred was that within the context of this relationship, certain issues in me began to surface that I never knew were there. I would have extreme emotional reactions to things that could have been handled differently and situations that were seemingly minor. There were so many internal things I needed to work on that after awhile I just couldn't ignore them any longer. That's when I believe the decision to mature and commit to my faith became so essential, because it was the start of that journey that helped me through some of those internal issues that I'd suppressed. It was at this point in my life that I began to chase a particular image (the image of a "Christian woman") that I believed would help counter the destructive image that I was living out at that point. My pursuit of this image was both a good and not-so-good thing. I believe it was a good thing because I had the sense of mind to know that I needed to put away old things in order to walk into the new. I realized that the old image that I had created for myself was doing me more harm than good. I would say that the pursuit was not so good because there is no such thing as the perfect image or the perfect template of a Christian woman. There is no such thing as the perfect image. We may have influence over our lives when it comes to things that we seek to adopt, but whenever we go chasing after an image, that image becomes an idol or even a counterfeit of our authentic true self. You will stifle yourself from actualizing your own potential. I thought I was pursuing God and I honestly believe that I was, but I was also pursuing the image of a perfect Christian woman, and unfortunately there is no such thing. The irony about my pursuit was that each and every one of my relationships—no matter how long- or short-lived—, always revealed just how imperfect I was. And I struggled with that.

As the years went on, I became the image of the mature Christian woman-or so I thought. I pursued a call to ministry simply because I felt like that was what someone like me was supposed to do. I know today that God has called me to certain unconventional areas of ministry, and I am finally confident in that, but ten years ago I pursued what I felt fit the image. I come out of a church tradition that places a great deal of emphasis on image: how you sound, how you preach, how you hoop, how long your skirt is, how to sit appropriately, how not to wear pants if you're a woman in the pulpit, how to carry yourself with poise so not to distract anyone with your humanity. I fell into the temptation of wanting everyone to accept me. I wanted to do things right, whether that was in my career, my lifestyle choices, or my personal relationships. I don't believe that I was being inauthentic or fake, but I do believe I wasn't reflecting who I truly was, probably because I wasn't seeking out my authentic self. That was not a part of me that I wanted people to see. When it came to men, I had this thing about wanting them to fall in love with my résumé and not me. I strategized about how I would prove to them that I was this accomplished, talented woman, and then I would get comfortable and show them me. I had this fear that if they saw me too soon, they would walk away. I didn't have a healthy understanding of who "me" was. If I truly loved and valued me, I would have realized that I was more than just a résumé or a set of gifts. I would have confidently presented the witty, intelligent, and often complicated me, along with all the other ingredients that make up who I am. The anointing can be very attractive, and many times we fall in love and want people to fall in love with our anointing and gifting and lose sight of the person underneath all of that.

It wasn't long before who I really was began to catch up with who I was trying to be. I believe that there was a part of me that began to evolve, and my true self wanted out of the prison that I had boxed myself into for so many years. And not only that, but there were parts of me deep down inside that really needed to grow up and change. Again, those parts of me always surfaced in the context of my relationships with men. Every time I would get hurt in one of those relationships, I would bottle it up and somehow hide how I was feeling or what was really happening because it didn't fit within the image I had constructed. My emotional reactions got worse and worse. Things would begin to pile up and eventually explode as I maneuvered my way through the cycles of dysfunction (such as in that situation I found myself in with that young man in seminary).

It wasn't until much later, when God opened a door for me to take a job in California, that someone would teach me the value of true friendship within the context of a relationship, even though we were not in a relationship. It was this same person who said to me about my previous situation: "Khristi, that wasn't a relationship." That was when I realized, "Oh gosh, no, it wasn't." Unfortunately that blossoming friendship was short-lived as well. I, for some reason, was looking to him to undo what the previous guy(s) had done. That wasn't his responsibility; it was mine. I didn't understand that I couldn't seek my healing from a relationship, no matter how good it was. I needed to seek healing from God. I needed to seek healing from myself, and I couldn't do that in a relationship. I needed to face these realities about myself:

> -I didn't understand how to be in a relationship.
> -I didn't understand that my denial was causing my emotional issues to pile up.

-I didn't understand that the way I coped with fear was that when it got triggered by something someone did or said, I would go into a rage because then I could control the wounded vulnerability that lay bare.

-I didn't understand that love didn't equate to dysfunction.

-I didn't understand that I needed to rid myself of keeping up with the "perfect" image because it wasn't allowing me the freedom to heal and evolve.

-I didn't understand that I was in a difficult process of becoming, and the image I was chasing was holding me back.

-I didn't understand that I could no longer keep up with the image.

It got to the point where I began self-diagnosing myself because I thought there must be something wrong with me. I actually went to my counselor and told her what I thought I had, when I was the one paying her to tell me. She would try to convince me that I was perfectly normal, yet I wasn't convinced. I had to have PTSD or GAD or some form of rejection sensitivity, and perhaps some of those symptoms were present, but I was obsessed with calling it something. It was in those counseling sessions that I realized I didn't have to be anyone but who I was. The majority of my life I had received the message (whether in relationships or in church or in other contexts) that I had to be a particular type of person. But now, in this space three thousand miles away from home, finally I began to realize that the message of true, unconditional acceptance that God was communicating to me and that my parents had instilled in me maybe wasn't a fluke at all. Here I would finally come into my own. It took some time to shed false images. It took some time to heal, simply because healing isn't a one-time event but an ongoing journey.

The Courage to Be

There is a movie starring Kathryn Heigl called *The Ugly Truth* where she plays a TV producer named Abby who is a single woman living in California. Abby is a rigid woman who believes in true love but has a particular idea of what the perfect man for her should look like. When she finally meets the man of her dreams, she in turn (with the help of a friend) proceeds to shift things about herself to make her more desirable to him. They change her hair, her style of dress, her behavior, her movements, and even how she responds to certain things. In the end she realizes that he only likes the woman that she had been pretending to be, not the real her. Disappointed, she breaks up with him.

I fear that many of us, male and female, have made the same mistakes as Abby. Whether in relationships, our careers, or other areas of our lives, we work tirelessly to be the image of who we think we should be as opposed to who we really are:

"He will love me more if_____."

"She will love me more if_____."
"They will accept me more if_____."

We all struggle with the image of who we really are alongside the images imposed by others onto us. The ugly truth is that there is no such thing as the perfect anything. This is a basic concept that we all know, but it's not often lived out in our language and in the messages that we communicate. We always seem to fall back into conformity. I was text messaging a friend and suggested he take a few days to relax as I noticed he was on the go quite a bit. He responded by saying that he wasn't going to relax and that he wants to be "a sexy eligible bachelor TD Jakes meets Tony Robbins with a hint of Les Brown." He went on to say that he also wants his body to be perfect so the "haters can hate." I responded by telling him that it was OK if he wasn't TD Jakes or Tony Robbins because he was enough. I encouraged him that there's nothing wrong with striving for greatness, but he can also discover extraordinariness within his own self.

In one of his most noted plays, Shakespeare asked, "To be or not to be, that is the question." It's a question we don't realize plays out in our everyday lives. There is a daily temptation to "be" or "not be" for the season, for that day, or even for that moment. To some people this phrase is as simple as choosing life or death, but being is more than just existing. Being is accepting who you are in spite of who you are. Being is exuding everything that makes up who you are, which includes the good and the bad:

every insecurity, every mistake, every gift, every talent, every success, every failure, every dream, every secret, every hope, and every fear, et cetera, et cetera. It's because of those contractions that many people lack the courage to be.[xvi] The courage to be is the act in which a person affirms his or her own being in spite of those elements of his or her existence that may conflict. It's not until we choose to confront ourselves and embrace ourselves with that courage that we will be better students, actors, daughters, sons, parents, musicians, scientists, artists, writers, leaders, and anything else. Courage is the unction that enables a person to face difficulty, danger, pain, and challenge without fear. Courage is the ability to move forward "in spite of."

Society is constantly pressuring us to be something or someone else other than who we are. It's not acceptable to just be 100 percent you and that be good enough. There is an old commercial where a young man is standing in the center of a room, and all of a sudden someone comes and puts a baseball cap on his head and then a coat. Then someone else comes and takes that cap off and puts on another cap and then another person comes and puts on another outfit. Then someone comes and puts a cigarette in his hands and earphones in his ears, and before you know it, there are dozens of people all around him putting things on him and taking things off of him. Finally he decides to push all the people away. He takes off all the clothing and items that were put on him and walks away by himself, wearing his own clothes. He decides at the end of the commercial that it was enough to just be him. Can you imagine all the layers our culture puts on us every day? We must act a certain way and dress a certain way and talk a certain way to be accepted. In every space you enter, there is a different set of unspoken rules, and we all find ways to conform.

Image is about projecting a visual standard. When you fall from that standard, you are reminded that you failed to reach that standard. Image can be a tricky concept, especially in a culture that places a great deal of emphasis on beauty, success, and acceptability by the masses. Image within the Christian culture can be just as tricky because we continually remind ourselves that we are sinful, imperfect beings in pursuit of a perfect God. But somehow we, too, have created a culture that places importance on acceptable imagery. We try to deny it by saying things like "come as you are," but somewhere along the line, that message changes to become as *we* are, speak as *we* speak, dress how *we'd* like for you to dress, and worship in a style that *we* have influenced you to. I've seen more examples of how the emphasis on image over integrity has done more harm than good. I have seen time and time again contradictions between leadership's personal "behind closed doors" integrity juxtaposed with their public image. We have created a tradition where we value the way things look in public more than we value personal integrity. Image is everything in the Christian community, and we need to stop pretending like it's not. I believe the emphasis that we place on image is the reason why many leaders take such great falls when the reality of their personal lives begins to catch up with the contradictory image they have projected.

Assigning Images

Our culture has a bad habit of assigning images to people, and to be honest, it's difficult not to. When you look at someone and you see that he went to a particular school, you automatically assign an image to him. If you see that someone is married to a particular person, then she is automatically assigned an image. If you hear that something happened in their life, you assign an image that agrees with what it is that you heard. Let's take Meagan Good for example. Meagan Good is a film and television actress known for sassy rolls that radiate with sex appeal. When she got engaged to and later married a well-known preacher and executive for Columbia Pictures named Devon Franklin, the critiques rolled in. Many people were confused by both his and her choice in marrying one another, because we all assigned an image to them that didn't fit. As a unit their marriage brings up and exposes a few issues pertaining to image assignment.

- What is a preacher's wife supposed to look like?
- Is it possible for one's image to evolve?
- Is it fair to place a former image on a present situation?
- What type of woman is a male preacher supposed to marry?

- How is a preacher's wife supposed to dress, behave, or carry herself?
- Can practicing believers be devoted to their faith in the entertainment industry while carrying out images that may differ with traditional images within the Christian culture?

I believe that they are great examples that bring out open-ended questions that need to be discussed within the Christian community. We have struggled with maneuvering through systems that we created to justify image assignment.

Many people associate image assignment with judgment. You often hear people say "don't judge me" when defending themselves against a conclusion that someone has drawn about them. However, judgment isn't always a bad thing. There is critical judgment as it relates to being a good judge of character. There is also authoritative judgment, which is concluded based on fact. In some cases, judgment is justified. The term *judgment* has been used subjectively when a person defends something that has been projected onto them. They resent being judged, even if that judgment is true. Therefore I do not like to use that word carelessly because sometimes it's warranted judgment. In the book of Matthew, Jesus said, "Do not judge or you will be judged." Many times it's this passage that people refer to when they think of judgment. However, I believe the focus of that entire passage was on accountability to self. Jesus did not want us to be so focused on other people that we did not apply that same level of attention on our own issues. It is clear throughout scripture that Jesus enacted critical judgment on those deserving of it, yet he also extended grace. I believe this version of the passage from the Message Bible is a clear delineation:

> **Matthew 7 1-5:** Don't pick on people, jump on their failures, criticize their faults—unless, of course, you want the same treatment. That critical spirit has a way of boomeranging. It's easy to see a smudge on your neighbor's face and be oblivious to the ugly sneer on your own. Do you have the nerve to say, "Let me wash your face for you," when your own face is distorted by contempt? It's this whole traveling road-show mentality all over again, playing a holier-than-thou part instead of just living your part. Wipe that ugly sneer off your own face, and you might be fit to offer a washcloth to your neighbor.

Consequently, "judging" and "assigning images" are terms similar in nature, but different. Assigning images to people is never acceptable, and we do it all the time.

Your Authentic Self

Self-discovery, identity, and authenticity need to be at the top of everyone's personal priority lists. It is only when we discover these things that we are capable of fulfilling our calls in this world, whether a calling in our careers, relationships, or life in general.

What's difficult is that we have to discover these things apart from systems and institutions that seek to define us within those spaces, and we have to define ourselves for ourselves. Author Audre Lorde once said, "If I didn't define myself for myself, I would be crunched into other people's fantasies for me and eaten alive." In the book *The Gift of Being Yourself*, David G. Benner suggests that in order to know God, we must know ourselves because in discovering ourselves we discover God. He highlights the idea that knowing God is an important part of Christian spirituality but knowing self is not as important of a notion. He concludes that

> Christian spirituality involves a transformation of the self that occurs only when God and self are both deeply known. Both, therefore, have an important place in Christian spirituality. There is no deep knowing of God without a deep knowing of self, and no deep knowing of self without a deep knowing of God.[xvii]

We must remove false selves, pay attention to ignored selves, study formed patterns, break free of dysfunctional cycles, and recover lost values. It starts with "majoring" in yourself, the way one would major in a field of study at school. We have to become that familiar with our intricacies. I knew a girl once who was told she was ugly her entire life and therefore thought she was ugly and carried herself that way. It wasn't until began her journey of self-discovery that she realized that she only thought she was ugly because she had been told she was ugly her entire life. I asked her one day, "Who told you that you were ugly?" And I continue to ask these kinds of questions when people are influenced by something or someone who had decided to impose conventions on individuals and deter them from their freedom of self. I say, "Who told you that you weren't capable? Who told you, young man, that you are not supposed to wear a hat in church? Who told you not to wear pants as a woman in the pulpit? Who told you that just because you had sex at some point, you are not pure in God's eyes? Who told you that you are not good enough?" When messages are communicated to us—defining who we are before we get a chance to discover who we are on our own—this causes a negative effect on ourselves and ultimately our culture. Many of us have concluded things about ourselves simply because someone told us that's the way it was. We have followed styles and patterns simply because someone told us that's the way it should be. We have not taken ownership over our freedom and our ability to make decisions and conclusions on our own. I understand the need for structure and appropriateness, but many times these structures suffocate the gospel of freedom and grace. Our families and our communities need us to be our whole, authentic selves, because there is something in the genuineness of who we are that will add value to our community.

Life should be looked at as a journey to discovering and accepting your true self, and that includes all the parts of you. I had to get to a point where I accepted not only the great and publicly acceptable parts of myself but also the challenging, shameful, and quirky parts as well. That is truly who I am. I will never be able to sustain a successful career—let alone a successful relationship—if I do not first embrace every single ingredient that makes up who I am. I had to stop chasing who I thought other people wanted me to be. I had to chase all that I am, and in turn I am finally able to get even a small glimpse of who God really sees. I am not the image of a perfect Christian woman, and I don't want to be. I am not the image of a perfect minister, and I don't want to be. I don't have the perfect Christian woman responses when somebody gets on my nerves, even though I am evolving. I don't like wearing dresses to church on Sunday; I like wearing flip-flops and jeans, although I understand when it's not appropriate to. I am a single Christian woman who has had a few sexual experiences. I am in counseling because I need it and I love my therapist, and I'll probably go to her for a long time because I need it. I am listing all of these things not so much for you, the reader, but for me to be able to see and affirm the fact that I am not perfect but I accept and am in love with who I am and who I'm evolving to be. I want to encourage you to do the same, because you will not be able to live the fullness of this life and live it abundantly chasing after images projected onto you by people and institutions who want you to fit within the context of what they want for you to be.

SINCERELY,
DIVORCED & MARGINALIZED

" Before I got divorced, without even realizing it, I had always been at the center of privilege being male, being Caucasian in predominantly Caucasian circles, and being ordained in ministry. That position put me at the center of decision making and power. After the divorce happened, I found myself suddenly at the margins of church life for the first time in my life. Part of that was because I was divorced. The church that I was at, if you were divorced—no matter what the reason—you were considered disqualified. So I was a "double D": I was disqualified and divorced. After I left there, I went around trying to find connection at other churches, and for the first time in my life, I found myself on the margins rather than at the center. It was very humbling and painful but what it did do was give me a tremendous amount of empathy for those who had been on the margins. For all those years, I wasn't even aware they were on the margins.

I went through quite a bit during that season personally. I went through a season of doubting. I knew I believed in Jesus and I knew I wanted to follow him, but everything else seemed as if it had collapsed onto the ground and I was trying to fit it back together again. At a certain point, I was just depressed and discouraged. I remember thinking, "If I lose my marriage but keep the ministry, I'll be OK" or "If I lose the ministry but keep the marriage, it will be really painful, but I think I'll be OK," but I didn't think I could survive losing both. There was a time all I did was part-time work. I didn't have a full-time job. I had joint custody of my kids. So half of my week I'd have my jobs and my kids and half the time I'd be alone. I could barely take a shower and get dressed in the morning.

There was a book club that a friend started, and eventually that became my strong sense of community that I sought. Half the people in the group were married, and the other half were unmarried. That immersed me in a Christian community that wasn't just comprised of people like me. We became a community regardless of marital status, political affiliation, ethnic diversity, and a bit of socioeconomic diversity. The only prerequisite was to be willing to ask difficult questions and not freak out if people were coming up with answers that were not your typical answers. Our affinity was that we were still believers and committed to following Jesus but were frustrated with the church background we had been a part of most of our lives. It started with a negative angst and eventually took a more solution-focused, positive turn.

There were two people from the book group-both single women who had never been married-who saw that I was going through a lot and began to reach out to me. They would say, "Hey, we're going out to dinner; come with us" or "We're going to see the Christmas lights; come with us." They were very intentional, and because they were best friends, there was no awkwardness that there may have been with one single woman asking me to hang out. The interesting thing about this is that they both are in their thirties and have stories where they have dated on and off but never connected with someone enough to form a long-term relationship. They are best friends and roommates. As a result people struggle to understand their friendship because it doesn't fit into the box of what we think a friendship should be. There is a constant chatter about them among family, church, and other circles, because there is no room in people's paradigm for individuals who are not married and not opposed to it but are not actively looking, either. They are simply friends who decided to do life together, and that doesn't fit. They have become some of the closest friends I have. Even after I remarried, my wife embraced them and loves them. Every summer we go camping together.

Now, as a married man, I can look at life through the vantage point of a person on the margins, whether it's someone unmarried or in a minority, even though I'm not there. My personal situation created an opportunity and ability for me to have more empathy than I had before.

Chapter 5

THE MYTH OF
THE ARRIVAL

"Once I meet my wife, then I can finally be happy."

I recently watched a documentary on ESPN about the legendary head coach of Tennessee, Pat Summit. The documentary was compelling, giving us a history of the life of Pat Summit as well as her determination and success in her career. The legacy that she will leave behind is that she is the winningest coach in college basketball history. She led the University of Tennessee Lady Volunteers to eight national championships and 1,098 victories. The most inspiring part of the documentary was when Pat Summit talked about how many Final Four trips her team took before they actually won a national championship. She said she would continue to reach the Final Four or make it to the championship game, and her team would lose. Because of this she started to question whether or not she was capable of ever winning a championship, because she would get so far and then not make it. She went on to say that her record of 1,098 victories was simply a result of coaching for twenty-seven years. Someone in the documentary commented that 1,098 victories also equated to a lot of losses. These moments spoke to me personally, because many times we assume that our failures, whether in our career or in our relationships, define us. We also assume that because we are not at a particular place in life and have not "arrived," then we will never get there. Pat Summit soon learned that arriving is all about the journey and that there is no such thing as getting to one place. Even after she would win a national championship, after cutting the net off of the basketball hoop, she would go back into the locker room and begin thinking and planning for the next year. I realized that this is what life is all about—the journey.

The Promised Land

There is a myth within our culture that projects the message that we have to get equipped because we have to arrive to someone. And while I understand the concept of preparation, I've come to realize that preparation is essential to becoming a whole person, regardless of your impending marital status. The idea is to be equipped for life and for where life will lead you, whether it's to another person or not—not to mention the fact that growing, learning, and evolving as a person continues even after one gets married. There is no such thing as "arriving" anywhere. There will always be new levels of learning and new levels of growing.

We should look at the different seasons in life as just another part of our journey. We should look at seasons as chapters.

The Promised Land imagery comes from the biblical story of Abraham, whose decedents were promised a land by God that would offer them the divine resources, joy, and stability of life that many of the Israelites hoped for. This imagery also shows up in American history at a time when hardships in other countries compelled many people to immigrate to the United States with the picture in mind that the United States was a sort of Promised Land. This land would offer them stability financially, personally, and emotionally that they needed to live a full life. Promised Land imagery also made an appearance in some of Dr. Martin Luther King Jr.'s speeches during the civil rights movement. He referred to the Promised Land metaphorically, suggesting that one day there would be a time in America when the races would be able to live together in peace and harmony. Dictionary.com also has another definition of Promised Land:

> *2. A place or situation in which someone expects to find great happiness.*

In the opening of this chapter, I quoted a phrase I have heard too often: "Once I meet my husband or wife, then I can finally be happy." If I meet a husband or a wife, then I can be happy: if this, then this. If I meet a husband or a wife, then I can begin my life. If I meet a husband or a wife, then I will have significance. If I meet a husband or wife, then I will be recognized. Someone asked me once if I was dating anyone or any closer to marriage, and when I responded "no," her response was "Oh, that's OK." To that I said, "Yes, it's more than OK." Then they said "Oh, you're still young." And to that I said, "What happens if I get older, and I'm not married? Does my life have any less significance?" The myth is that there are conditions behind ultimate happiness and inclusion in the community. Therefore the message sent is again, echoed in Katelyn Beaty's article that I quoted in an earlier chapter, "You must have this in order to be a complete human being."[xviii] This is a lie. Life begins at conception and evolves in many beautiful stages, some having to do with marriage and others not. The marriage as "a Promised Land" strips individuals of their right to live an abundant life in their present states.

In John 10, Jesus speaks of the fullness of the life he has to offer:

> [10] The thief's purpose is to steal and kill and destroy. My purpose is to give them a rich and satisfying life.
>
> (New Living Translation)

> [10] The thief does not come except to steal, and to kill, and to destroy. I have come that they may have life, and that they may have *it* more abundantly.
>
> (New King James)

[10] The thief comes only to steal and kill and destroy; I have come that they may have life, and have it to the full.

(New International Version)

On a basic level, this passage can be interpreted as Jesus saying that through him is the life of eternal salvation, joy, peace, and strength. Others have taken this a step farther, teaching messages that interpret this passage to mean that God wants us to have material things and to have an abundance of greater blessings and privileges. While I don't argue with those delineations, I tend to believe this passage means that God wants us to live out our freedom and live it abundantly. If we are, in fact, free in Christ, then our freedom is not bound to traditional means of happiness. I believe that it means abundant living within our freedom, and this means something different for every person. A major theme in Jesus's teaching was freedom: freedom from institutional bondage, stereotypes, human judgment, traditional ways of thinking, and many others. Therefore, a great deal of what Jesus taught and how Jesus lived and moved was founded on guiding individuals toward true life. The myth of the arrival contradicts this freedom. I don't need anything else outside of him to have the abundant, full life that Christ speaks of. While the Christian community lectures that all one needs is Jesus, it preaches an inherent contradiction that one falls short if he or she isn't living this life out with a husband/wife and children. The contraction is that while Jesus may offer full life, this is the only way to a fuller life.

The Exclusive Club

Another harmful effect of the arrival myth is the prevalence of pride and exclusivity among those who have "arrived." It's the mentality that the Israelites adopted in the Bible after finally reaching their "Promised Land."[xix] It's a story my colleagues and I wrestled with in the beginning of my seminary training. After the Israelites had been enslaved to the Egyptians for so many years, once they were finally free, it took them forty years of preparation in order to get to their promised land. The part of scripture that we struggled with was the idea that the land that they were entering into was full of people, much like themselves, that they were instructed to conquer and destroy. The command to kill all the Canaanite people was disturbing because it seemed at odds with the likeness of God. It's a story that we never quite reconciled, though we managed to maintain a sturdy faith. However, many questions surfaced in my mind in regards to the Israelites and their conquest. Had they forgotten the pain of *their* land being taken from them? Had they forgotten the struggles of elongated preparation? Had their memories been so wiped away with the temptation of finally arriving that they, in turn, demeaned those who were in the positions they were in not long before?

One of my closest friends recently participated in her cousin's wedding. My friend was one of the most supportive bridesmaids you'd ever come across. She planned and celebrated bridal showers and dinners. She catered to her cousin at every moment, even during the challenging ones. Once the wedding ceremony came, the day was filled with beauty and expectation. My friend stood in agreement with the union between her cousin and her new husband proudly. She recalls a moment at the end of the ceremony, right before the bride walked back down the aisle with her husband. She leaned toward my friend and said, "Don't worry, girl, you're next. You are going to get there." My friend wondered to herself, "Get where exactly?" Had my friend's cousin arrived somewhere that we all should strive to be? When she told my friend not to worry, did she assume that she was in a state of despair just because she was single?

The battle for recognition and status is a predicament in the Christian community. It's also an oxymoron. In a faith where "the first shall be last and last shall be first" and where the Messiah lived modestly, born in a manger and riding confidently on donkeys, the message of self-denial and our culture's constant need for classification contradict. The temptation to separate groups of people and label them as important or not important is a constant tendency within our culture. Therefore, the "single" and "married" designation often gets exaggerated in excessive ways. Much like the traditional bouquet or garter toss in wedding ceremonies, our culture has communicated a message that often takes on the image of a country club. If a country club is a private club, often with a closed membership, what kind of message is that sending to women and men who are single? Many people would do anything to receive status or recognition within our culture. As a result, they would do almost anything to be a part of desirable subcultures, just to be included. I truly believe that a beautiful, healthy marriage with a life partner is something that many people can desire. However, the "club membership" notion can be damaging, simply because it's divisive. People use club and team language, thinking that it's harmless, when in actuality it projects an "I'm in and you're not" message. The only team we should be recruiting people for is the team of Jesus Christ, who again, sought to redefine family by creating an all-inclusive kingdom whose membership is open enrollment. When speaking of her experience with other single friends in the church who began to get married, one woman I interviewed said: "People would spin off and marry one another, and then they would disappear and you would never hear from them again. It was like we weren't even friends for two years. Like we did all this stuff together, we hung out and barbequed, and it was like 'Oh, now I'm married, and I'm in a different club now.'"

It's not to say that married people don't need space to come into their self-identity. But, the exclusiveness is disheartening and divisive.

Growing up, my school district was very serious about athletics. As a result, high-school and junior high-school coaches would put on two-day clinics in the middle school to scout potential athletes. There was a group of athletic young girls who caught the attention of these coaches, and I was one of them. They groomed us in the summers during our seventh- and eighth-grade years, and by the time ninth grade came around, we had an opportunity to try out for the high-school team. Our junior high school consisted of eighth and ninth grades, even though ninth grade is technically high school. It was almost a shoo-in who would get chosen to play for the junior varsity high school team. I thought I was included in that group. Unfortunately they had only a certain number of spots, and I was the only one left on the junior high team, while the others who I had worked with for the past three years were bused every day after school to the high school practices. I was devastated. I didn't make the team. It was torture going to school following the announcement, when everyone would give me pitied looks and have awkward conversations with me about what happened. I remember feeling excluded. I remember feeling embarrassed. I remember feeling singled out. My friends were a part of a team I wasn't good enough to make. This unfortunately is a reflection of how Christian culture segregates the "teams" of marrieds and singles.

I know of a person who would do almost anything to get off "team single." He is literally dating any and everyone who will say yes in order to finally be married. From the outside looking in, I know that this person's desperation comes from his involvement in a community of people who continue to pressure him to hurry up so that he can finally be a part of what they all share in common. Unfortunately the long-term effects of this "join our club" mentality is that it clouds one's judgment when it comes to making a thoughtful, prayerful decision when it comes to partnering with another person in life.

I had conversation with another friend shortly after his divorce. He had been with his ex-wife for less than two years. When he began to evaluate all of the things that went wrong, he pointed out character flaws and things that he felt were intolerable. I was confused because he said they had dated for a year before they were engaged. I couldn't understand why he had never noticed those things when they were dating. He said he felt pressured by the church because people pushed him to get married. He felt that his ex-wife wanted to get married quickly because she was getting older. He said those messages stifled his ability to really process those things that bothered him. He said it didn't matter then because of all of the hysteria. My friend's marriage is a casualty of the hyperpressurized concept of marriage at any cost for the sake of cultural inclusion. The mentality is that one must arrive in order to arrive.

"The Right Way"

Once upon a time, I imagined that when I got into a relationship and was married, I could then tell people "how I did it." I thought I could share with them how I, too, had arrived. That was wrong thinking. I use the celebrity couple Will and Jada Pinkett Smith as an example. In spite of the fact that their marriage and style of governing their family has been criticized, Jada has made it clear that this is the method they have chosen to make their family work. It may not be everyone's cup of tea, but she is very clear that while she may share lessons and wisdom she has learned with other people, they are not universal instructions. When people who are married exude dispositions of "arrival," sometimes the temptation to impart a superior wisdom into others who have not "arrived" is hard to resist. Instead of making suggestions and offering lessons learned, they try and guide others to be more like them, emulating a false perfection. Again, this has damaging effects.

I once heard a story about a man and his wife who said that they thought they had a great marriage until they started reading books on how to have a great marriage. He said once that happened, they attempted to do what the books told them to do, and that's when their marriage began to suffer. I'm not saying that books on marriage are not useful. On the contrary, I feel as though self- and couple-help books are beneficial to the growth of a relationship. However, when the idea communicated is a "do what I do" as opposed to a guide, it can be detrimental. I'm always concerned with people who communicate a message that somehow they got it right and we are all to follow their suit. I understand that we can glean from people's experiences, but to say that somehow one particular couple has discovered the panacea for all marriages is unethical. There is no right way. I've come to grow a profound respect for couples who say that they have chosen what works for them and are open to sharing wisdom they've acquired with others.

Shaming

Someone close to me once asked, "When are you going to hurry up and get married?" I responded, "Maybe never. I may just be single. And would that be a bad thing?" That completely threw him off. I imagine that all of these questions popped up in his head: What will she do for sex? Would she dare have it outside of marriage? How will she ever be happy? What does a smart, pretty, woman do with herself if she's not married and having kids?

These are questions that most single people get all the time. These are the questions they want to avoid at family gatherings. There's always that one aunt or uncle who wants to know why they're not popping babies out. These are the questions that make you cringe at church when people want to pry into your dating life. I like to refer to it as "marriage shaming." Marriage shaming is when an individual or group pressures a woman or man into guilt because of her or his relationship status.

> **Shame**- *n.* **1. a.** A painful emotion caused by a strong sense of guilt, embarrassment, unworthiness, or disgrace.

Marriage shaming can be intentional or unintentional. I tend to believe that the majority of the time it is unintentional. Because it is so much a part of our culture, people who have adopted this behavior aren't aware that it is harmful. Marriage shaming can be as direct as someone slighting another because he or she is not married, or as indirect as being in an environment where married or engaged couples are at the center of regard and acceptance. I don't believe anyone in the Christian community likes to openly admit to being guilty of shaming anyone.

Just the other day my friend and I were talking about a young woman with whom we were friends with in years past. I said to my friend, "I wonder why she's not married," and my friend said, "Girl, I'm not surprised." I responded in agreement, as though to place blame on our friend's persona as the reason she wasn't married. I had to check myself later. I, too, had fallen into the temptation of marriage shaming.

It is furthermore clear that women are more commonly victims of marriage shaming than men. When men are single past a certain age, they are classified as bachelors. When women are, they are associated with being old maids. When men are single past a certain age, they are making choices for their lives and living to the fullest until they "settle down." When women are single past a certain age, something must be wrong with them. I see the double standard with men and women, but I cannot ignore the fact that men feel the same pressure at times. Shaming is contradictory to the foundational principles that our Christian community stands on. This reluctance to admitting transgressions, whether intentional or unintentional, is part of the reason why our general culture has such a hard time moving forward in regards to discussions on race and ethnicity. Offending parties typically resent accusations of being something that they pride themselves on not being. Likewise, many people within our culture don't like to confront the reality behind the bigotry of marriage shaming, even though they may not realize they're doing it. I don't believe anyone who's ever asked me why I am not married was ever out to intentionally harm me. At the same time, I don't believe that many churches that I've been in who have placed married couples at the center of power were intentionally trying to exclude me. Whatever the intent, ignorance still requires correction.

There are other types of shaming as well that are not just limited to single individuals. For example: baby shaming. I know of many couples who don't have children for a variety of reasons. Some couples have a hard time having a baby; other couples have just chosen not to have children for one reason or another. The baby shaming begins with the question "When are you going to have a baby?" People make comments about your eggs drying up. They say that you're running out of time. Parents want to know when you're going to give them grandchildren. In this day and age, when so many things are out of our control, those types of interrogations are unfair. I know someone who really wants to get pregnant and has suffered multiple miscarriages. If I didn't know her and I approached her with the infamous "When you going to hurry up and have a baby?" question, that would hurt her. I know of another woman and her husband who just don't want to have kids. They don't mind their nieces and nephews, but they have made the decision as a couple not to have children because they want to live a particular lifestyle. The amount of shame and judgment that these two receive is remarkable. There's stay-at-home mom or dad shaming, when people look down on someone who decides to serve his or her family domestically. There's divorce shaming, when we look down on people who have been divorced without knowing their situations. We are supposed to exude grace-giving as a community, yet we have chosen only the acceptable areas to give grace in. Overall, shaming a person because he or she does not fit within the "traditional mold" is anti-gospel. It is a part of our culture that needs to shift.

Living in Freedom

Two of my married friends, on two separate occasions, asked me, "Girl, do you even want to get married?" These questions came as a result of them seeing me travel, make films and plays, and hang out in the city at night with friends. They ask me this because they see me pursuing the things of life and not spending all of my time pursuing one man. They automatically assume that because my life doesn't consist of attending singles nights, asking friends to hook me up, and sitting at home, twiddling my thumbs and waiting for the phone to ring, that I don't want to get married. That's not the case. I want to get married, but I also want to be careful. I want to get married, but I also want to use wisdom. I want to get married, but I also want to maintain a healthy sense of self. One of my friends even said to me recently that I wasn't going to find the love that I'm searching for traveling as much as I do. This was such a loaded statement, because, for starters, I was wondering how he assumed I was on a treasure hunt for love.

Secondly, how would my traveling restrict me from coming across a romantic interest? I would think it would increase it. Lastly, I've never ever heard that sort of message communicated to a man. On the contrary, most men are often encouraged to travel and live in freedom and move toward self-discovery.

In the first chapter, I mentioned that part of the call to singleness is a call to individual freedom. Earlier in this chapter I suggested that living out this freedom is a part of the fullness of life that Christ has called us to. I believe in terms of freedom: one can live out freedom in his or her singleness and live out a differently defined freedom in marriage. For the purpose of this book, my argument is that living out one's freedom in singleness is essential to whole personhood. Living out this freedom is defined differently for each person based on his or her passions, gifts, and, many times, desires. Within the framework of living out one's desires, this message has often been communicated in relation to sexual desires. It is typically a message projected onto men in regard to living free in their sexuality before they get tied down in marriage. However, living out freedom is multifaceted. I once had a friend who acquired an interest in weightlifting and competing in figure competitions. One day she decided to train to compete. She devoted her life to training, and for about six to eight months she worked out, was on a regimented diet, and had strict sleeping patterns. This decision cost her not only a great deal of time and energy, but it was expensive as well. Many people, including myself, were uncomfortable with this decision. We wondered why she was wasting her time and money. However, this was a decision that she made for herself that she owned, and she ultimately wound up being quite successful. She was not married at the time, she did not have children, and this is how she chose to spend her time, energy, and money. This was how she chose to live out her freedom in that season of her life. I remember a time not too long ago when I decided to join a women's basketball league. I played basketball all through my adolescence and thought it would be fun to play again, meet new people, and compete at a different level. I remember telling someone that I joined the league, and this person's response was "Oh, you just need to hurry up and get married." His comments suggested that because I had nothing better to do—like have a husband and kids—my decision to join this league was one out of desperation. We have to stop judging people and their freedom in their singleness. It's natural to see someone doing a lot of different things and automatically default to thinking that they are all over the place when in actuality they are just living out their freedom. People will pressure others to settle down and lead a "normal" life, but the reality is you don't have to. I've heard stories of people in leadership positions telling someone who's single to hold off on moving forward with their education and career and that she should focus on becoming a good wife instead. This is harmful advice. Why would someone want to willingly put her life on hold for something circumstantial? Our goal should be to pursue life. Pursue education, travel the world, take up a passion or hobby, start a book club, audition, direct a film, write a book, go to a concert, et cetera. These are not merely things to do in your "spare time" but helpful ingredients for a full life. It is your life and your freedom. I encourage men and women, no matter what age you are, to live out your freedom. There are no rules to what a so-called normal life should look like. Therefore we have to resist a culture that endeavors to define one for us. The journey toward self-discovery is a never-ending one. You will never stop being you or stop being who you are just because you arrive at a different season in life. Therefore, you cannot afford to wait to live out freedom until you get to a particular place. Freedom is already at our disposal. In the words of Tori Kelly's song "Confetti":

> People seem to think that you'll be happier
> once you reach the top
> You'll have it all; But I'm living for right now,
> 'cause what if tomorrow never comes.
> I'm not waiting for the confetti to fall.

SINCERELY, FULL LIFE

    ❝ Something that I have thought about a lot is the scriptures that actually speak highly of singleness and say that the man or woman who is married is devoting him or herself to his or her spouse and the person who is single is able to devote him or herself totally to God. I enjoy getting to do that, and that is something you never hear in church. You never hear that there's something amazing and great about being able to have that freedom. I'm going to Uganda in two and a half weeks. I teach math at a local university, but the last two summers I've taken short-term mission trips to Uganda. It occurred to me that I'm eligible for a sabbatical, and why not take a sabbatical in Uganda? So I arranged last summer to fly there a day before the rest of the team and meet with the math department, and it went really well. I applied for the sabbatical when I got back, and they accepted it. I'll be working at a university called Makerere University, and I am very excited. I will have a house sitter at my home, and I will get paid from my university job here. The university has a guest house, and it looks like I'm going to stay there the whole time. It's probably a little fancier than I would want, but it will work out. When I first get there, a friend of mine and my mom are coming, and we're going to do a little bit of ministry and visit some of the places I've been the past two years. Once the academic year starts, I will have to see what develops. I know people at a few churches there, so I have some connections. It's weird but the Sabbath aspect of it will be good for me because I haven't slowed down in a long time. It sounds backward because I'm going to be teaching and taking an online class and doing whatever ministry I can, but it's still going to be slowing down for me.

I know I will fall in love with it. A lot of people think I will end up moving there for good, and it's not that I would mind doing that, but I don't feel called to live there permanently. I do feel that taking people to Uganda for short trips will be a part of my life for a long time. If I was married and had kids, maybe I'd be driving to soccer, but instead I'm doing the kinds of things that I can do to make my own contributions to this world. Even my life here in California wouldn't be possible if I was married, because I teach full-time at the university, I go to school part-time, and I'm in ministry a great deal, and there's no way I could do all those things. It's borderline too much, but it's just for this season. I love being able to have this crazy season. It seems like a lot of Christians grow up with the perfect picture given to them by their churches of marriage and having a family. It's been awhile since I've dated. I'm actually forty years old even though people think I'm ten years younger. People still try and set me up with people, but it hasn't ended up going anywhere. And I guess theoretically I am open to it; I think it would be amazing. I think it would be great to be married if it was something healthy, but I would want that person and that relationship to add to my life. I enjoy my full life, and I would want someone to join in with that.

Chapter 6

THE MYTH OF THE PHRASE "BEING MARRIED TO JESUS"

"I am not single, I am taken. I am married to Jesus."

It is clear that our culture has conveyed a message that authentic connectedness can occur only within the context of a relationship with another man or woman. And for those awkward moments when one happens to be single past a certain time…Well then, don't worry, because you are "married to Jesus." I'm not sure when this phrase originated. My personal beliefs are that as we have moved into the new millennium, statistics regarding marriage have fluctuated. The estimated median age for women and men getting married is between twenty-seven and twenty-nine years old. The rate of divorce has also risen considerably, and values have shifted when it comes to perceptions of marriage. Therefore, the Christian community has a larger subculture of singles than in times past. Since marriage is at the core of our community's values and a large percentage of us are single, there have been two responses: 1) Hurry up and get all the single people married, and 2) Give the singles a quick, temporary response for their inconvenient position. I believe that it was out of this the idea emerged that while married people are married to each other, single people are married to Jesus.

Double Meaning

What does this mean exactly? On one hand, the intention behind the "married to Jesus" concept is a sound one. It's a notion that suggests that our priority as people of faith should lie in our relationship with Jesus Christ. It implies that God should be our primary source of love and acceptance. At the heart of the message is a healthy idea that we should not assume marriage will meet our unmet needs, but rather we should trust and rely on the resources of Christ. On the other hand, the idea of being married to Jesus has some major flaws that have left more people feeling awkward and uncomfortable than embracing its core intended value.

It's a Secondary Response

A major problem is that being "married to Jesus" has become a secondary response. It is as though I'm married to Jesus—if all else fails. There was a time in my early twenties when I would say that I was taken or in a relationship when I wasn't just to ward off men I wasn't interested in. Only then was I conveniently married to Jesus. When someone approached me who I was inter-ested in, then I was completely available. It all depended on the situation. Other times I was married to Jesus when I was tired of getting asked questions about being single. Someone would ask me, "When are you going to get married?" and I would reply that I was, because I was married to Jesus. However, when I was in a relationship with a guy, being married to Jesus never crossed my mind. Yes, Jesus and I were still in a relationship, but it was different.

How many times have you heard someone in a relationship or marriage talking about being married to Jesus? You may hear it, but it's seldom and most assuredly not the first response when someone asks if he or she is in a relationship. This is problem-atic because as Christians our relationship with God should be at the center of our faith. Moving Jesus around from one convenient position to another is unfair to Jesus. People who are single don't need to default to "being married to Jesus" as a means of escaping the uncomfortable reality of admitting that they are flying solo in life. It is overcompensation.

The Guilt Trip

In her article, "What Not to Say to Singles," Debra K. Fileta discussed her issues with the phrase "being married to Jesus" and her perception of its effects on single people:

> I'm amazed that people actually say this stuff. But accord-ing to the emails I get from singles across the nation—it's

a phrase that is being uttered to single men and women and is causing some major damage. The problem with this idea is that it leaves singles with a whole lot of guilt that they were never intended to feel. When singles are asked to be okay with being "married to Jesus" it makes them view their desire for marriage as a sign that they aren't okay with Jesus.[xx]

People used to tell me that it's good that I'm single because this way I can just focus on Jesus. This always confused me because I wondered why Jesus would get shortchanged if I got married. At the same time, I agree with Fileta in her assessment that just because someone wants to be in a relationship doesn't mean that his or her desire is a sign of discontentment with Christ. I often hear people use Philippians 4: 11-12 to brashly remind people who are single to be content.

11 I am not saying this because I am in need, for I have learned to be content whatever the circumstances. 12 I know what it is to be in need, and I know what it is to have plenty. I have learned the secret of being content in any and every situation...

This scripture was written as a tool to encourage people to be content in their present states, but I have seen it used to make people feel guilty about their desires. Just because they have desires doesn't mean that they are not content in their current state or relationship with God. However, the question always remains:

can one be content and still have these desires? My answer would be yes. I agree that we all should strive to be at peace in whatever situation we find ourselves in. At the same time, I believe that we should encourage people to talk through and embrace their desires. There's nothing wrong with wanting to be in a relationship. It's perfectly normal, even for the content single Christian.

Other Questions

Are only women married to Jesus because it's heterosexually acceptable? Can men say they're married to Jesus, and that would be acceptable?

Are people in relationships married to Jesus too, or only single people?

Is there an age restriction on being married to Jesus? Can a ten-year-old say she's married to Jesus, and it would be acceptable?

Even though scripture refers to the body as "the Bride of Christ," Jesus himself was never married. How do we reconcile that?

DTR

One of my friends recently shared with me about the transition he had to make from being a married man to a divorced man. He told me that for a good part of his life, he had all of his pieces in order. He said that he was growing as a man of God and growing as a husband. He said that he confidently knew his place in this world and in the church as well as in his career; however, when he got divorced, things began to shift. His perception of life, ministry, and personhood were all rocked. He felt guilt and anguish and had a hard time connecting with his faith through this experience. He told me that he soon came to realize that he needed to redefine his relationship with Christ. He knew what it meant to have a relationship with Jesus as a married man with a comfortable lifestyle; however, he didn't know what it meant to serve Christ in his current state. Essentially, he needed to do a DTR, which means "define the relationship." What did it mean for him—a divorced male feeling isolated, alone, struggling with his faith, and not connecting to the community around him—to have a relationship with Christ? It was different in that particular season of his life.

At that point I had to ask myself, "What does it mean for me, as a thirty-one-year-old single woman immersed in a new environment in California, to have a relationship with Christ?" I knew what it meant to serve Jesus as a teenager living in a comfortable context with my family. Once I entered into college, I had to define it once again, asking myself what it meant to have a relationship with Christ as a semi-independent college student growing into young adulthood. After college I needed to do the same thing, as this redefining continuously took place during the various cycles of life. This is the approach that I believe we need to take with everyone in the church as opposed to scapegoating with "married to Jesus" responses. We need to encourage singles in their various seasons of life to reflect on what it means to be in relationship with

Jesus Christ in the state they're in. What does it mean for someone divorced? Widowed? Going to college? Newly married? Moving into a second decade of marriage? Moving into a new career? So, it's not that you're single and married to Jesus, but rather, you're single and have a unique relationship with Christ in this season. This type of diverse experience in relationship is what the church needs, because we are not all at the same place. We are not at the same places in our faith journeys. I've heard many people advise singles to spend time with married couples so that they will learn from them, but I also encourage singles and even married people to spend time with singles who are at different stages in life. I sat with a single woman who was transitioning in her life, moving to another country to work at a hospital, and I learned a great deal from her experience. When I talked to my divorced friend, I learned from his season of faith struggles because the reality is, we will all be there. I learn from my married friends about the various stages in their married lives. Therefore, clumping singles and marrieds into two groups and assuming all are the same is foolish. We need each other's Jesus experiences, because we are all married to Jesus.

Reason and Response

Sometimes we feel as though we have to provide reasons for people being single. We say that someone *has* to be single because of _____. If they're single and pretty, they're not married because they are too focused on their career. If they're single and cute, they're not married because they're unstable. If they're single and educated, they're not married because they're too educated. If they're just plain ol' single, they're not married because they're crazy. In turn, we'll come up with excuses as to why they are single and then come up with formulas as to how to get them unsingle. I went out with this guy on one date and when I came back to tell a friend about it, I shared with her how I was so focused on my projects that I wasn't particularly looking for anyone. I told her that I was happy to be asked out and had been thrown off that he asked because I didn't notice that he was interested. Her response was "Yep, that's how it happens. It always happens when you're not looking." Even though she meant differently, that seems to be many people's formula for when and how romantic love can take place in someone's life. The theory is that it will happen when you're not looking. However, I know of plenty of people who actively pursued a relationship, met someone, and are married now.

There are many other things we suggest single people do. We tell them that they should make a list and pray over the list. We tell them that they're married to Jesus and they should just keep their focus there until God brings them someone. We tell them that they should fast and pray for their spouses (which I agree with) and then after that, they will appear. We tell them that if they focus on (this particular thing), then their spouse will come. An old friend of mine got so sick of the formulas put on her by the Christian community that she decided one day to start dating multiple men at once. She did this for a few years until she narrowed it down and decided to marry one of them. Even though this isn't a style I would lean toward in my personal choices, I can feel the pain of her growing frustration with the rules, reasons, and magic formulas she'd been presented her entire life. People are just putting their personal experiences on others when they share formulas with them. Again, I believe that suggestions are great. I believe that experiences can be gleaned from. But to tell a person that there is one way something is going to occur just because it happened to you or someone else is deceiving. There is no magic formula to life.

Worse than Being Alone: Worse than Being Married

A friend recently shared with me a Facebook status that he put on his personal page where he mentioned that in spite of the successful place that he was in life, it was still difficult waking up to an empty bed in the morning. I appreciated his transparency and have often found myself sharing the same sentiment. For the most part, I've noticed that people want to journey through life with a partner. Desiring to be married is just as healthy as being content in one's singleness. Desiring to share the wonder and complexities of life with another person is completely normal. Conversely, I fear that we have normalized it so much that we have created a standard that authentic community only comes through this type of a relationship.

We have normalized it so much that we have excluded a rather large subculture of people who live life without a partner. I don't believe that we need to get rid of the phrase "being married to Jesus," but rather redefine what being married to Jesus was truly means.

Another friend, who happens to be single, gave me the best insight when it comes to this subject:

> I fell in love with integrity early on. All my natural tendencies and hormones were always to find a really attractive girl and hang on to her. But even though this may sound a bit superficial, I always thought that if it was better to be single then I was going to learn how to be comfortable being single. At the time it was kind of ignorant, but now I've been thinking that discipline for me worked to my advantage. It forced me to think about where I'm going to find my real joy and peace. Pursuing God has allowed me to be completely at peace just being in a relationship with God. Even if I didn't have my career or a relationship, just knowing God and being in a relationship with God gives me peace. I never want to lose that, whether I get married or not. That is what I always want my life's foundation to be about. If you're in a relationship and you have that peace, you have so much more to offer, and if you're single and you have that peace, then you have so much more to offer to the community around you.

When we pursue a relationship with Christ, he fulfills an ultimate relationship void that we will never be able to have in another human being. When we seek God first, we open ourselves to a relationship with the creator of all existence. We intently join ourselves with the only one who can reveal to us our true identities. If being married means being permanently joined together, then a joining together with Christ is something that I should desire, no matter what state I find myself in. I could have the most expensive wedding ring, the biggest wedding, the largest home, and a husband to wake up to every day, but if the presence of God is absent and if my relationship with Christ is nonexistent, then that would be worse than being married or being alone. A few nights ago, I was listening to a song by gospel artist J. Moss called "Abundantly." The words of the chorus jumped out at me:

> Never wanna sleep without you. Never wanna wake without you. Never wanna part with life abundantly. Never take a chance without you. Never do my best without you. Never want to leave this life abundantly.

I had to ask myself what would be worse than sleeping alone. This connection is what I am married to. Jesus Christ is who I never want to be separated from. I always want to be joined together to him. That's the place we need to get to in our faith journeys: the place where our commitment to Christ is unshakable, regardless of the stage at life we're in.

The Marriage of Self

In spite of a universal call to a relationship with Christ, I believe that the focus for the single person should be on the marriage of self. It is the marriage of your "tri-part," which I mentioned in chapter one: body, soul, and spirit. If those three are not in conjunction with one another, then you are not functioning as a complete person. Single people have the privilege and responsibility to come into their well-established individuality, whether they get married or not. What we have to seek to pursue is wholeness within ourselves. We have to marry our "being" so that we can be complete persons. To marry yourself you have to love yourself enough to invest in those areas. You may have heard the phrase "You must first learn how to love yourself." This concept can be a bit obscure, unfortunately, because it doesn't come with an instruction manual. I believe that this, too, has become yet another clichéd phrase that many people resort to when they run out of advice to give to someone who is single. At the same time, I completely understand the necessity of the concept. Loving yourself begins with having a healthy perspective of the whole self: body, soul, and spirit. Self-love can come only when you realize your worth and value and pay attention to these areas. Once this happens, you will do whatever it takes to nurture your body, soul, and spirit in order to grow and protect these areas to evade the potential for harm.

I am at a point in my life where I can spot the potential for a damaging and harmful relationship from a mile away. Of course it has come through my fair share of painful situations, but it's more than just lessons learned. I truly love myself enough to not willingly walk into dysfunction. I love myself enough to not sacrifice my well-being or the things that I know I deserve for the sake of being able to say that I have someone. I literally had to retrain my way of living and thinking because for so long I had been attracted to dysfunction and calling it love. I knew that my perception of self was off, because I had consistently taken the "sacrificial lamb" disposition within relationships instead of the copartner, friendship motif. Not only did I pray that God would change my heart, but I had to break cycles and patterns of dysfunction in order to be able to clearly perceive what a healthy relationship would look like. It started with me taking a good look in the mirror and asking myself if I really, truly loved me. If so, then why would I willingly invite harmful situations? I had to ask myself why I was neglecting my spirit. I lacked investment in my emotional well-being. I didn't care for my body. I needed to recommit myself to myself. The journey toward self-love was one where a marriage needed to take place within myself. My spirit, mind, will, emotions, and body needed to be joined together as one. It wasn't about me grabbing Jesus as my husband as a means of saying I had someone. I needed to grab a hold of myself.

In his book *The Gift of Being Yourself*, David Benner says,

Before we can surrender ourselves we must first become ourselves, for no one can give up what he or she does not first possess. Jesus puts it this way: "If you're content with simply being yourself, you will become more than yourself." (Luke 18:14, The Message). Before we can become ourself we must accept ourself, just as we are. Self-acceptance always precedes genuine self-surrender and self-transformation.[xxi]

Love between two people is something to be celebrated. Love within one's self is just as congratulatory. We need to begin encouraging and celebrating the individuality of people who are single. As they move toward becoming more whole, self-accepting, and self-loving, we should rejoice that we have another healthy person to contribute greatness to the world around us. We need to remind singles that their individuality is valuable to this world, in or outside of the context of marriage. Singleness is not a basis for self-doubt; it is a badge of honor and something to be esteemed. Don't let anyone devalue you (even playfully) by constantly badgering you about when you going to get married. You don't have to respond and say that you're married to Jesus as an excuse. You are a single individual walking in wholeness, serving Christ and those around you. Point. Blank. End of subject.

SINCERELY, WOMAN IN MINISTRY

❝ In 2003 I was preparing to be licensed and was dating someone who was my best friend. He was OK with my call to ministry initially. We both went back to school and spent a great deal of time together, going out and working alongside one another in a local school district. In 2004 he wanted to get married, but I wasn't ready. It had nothing to do with ministry. It was just the whole thought of getting married at twenty-three was laughable. It's like, "I'm not going to submit to you. I'm struggling to submit to God." So it was laughable. The first time we had that conversation, he was a little upset, but it was OK. Everything was just fine until 2005 when I started preaching more. I was also serving at another church locally. I was traveling back and forth within that state and other states to preach. We could never just go to church and sit together, and he wondered why we couldn't just be normal and attend and sit together. But I was a clergywoman, and normal for me was that in the context of a church, I serve. He felt church should be a family thing, and we should go to church and sit together, but with me, I sat in the pulpit. So ministry became an issue, and the traveling became an issue. Also, as time went on, other issues arose. When you date someone for a certain period of time and you're a Christ follower, after a while they are wondering, what more? If marriage is not the next step, then what is? We had maxed out. We got as intimate as we could without being physically intimate. I wasn't going for it because I couldn't compromise in that particular area. He agreed that he couldn't compromise me, but I didn't know at the time he was messing with other girls.

In 2005, Christmas Day, I was asked to move to another state. One of the pastors asked me to join staff full-time. This was something I knew I was called to. At the same time, my boyfriend wanted to get married again. I thought I was definitely ready at this time. But for some reason, when he asked, I was hesitant. I told my boyfriend that I couldn't say yes. I felt like God was telling me no. I couldn't say yes, but I didn't know what that meant. He was upset, and then I left to take the position. Fast-forward about a month, and I get a phone call from a girl, who tells me that she had been sleeping with my boyfriend. She knew all about me. She knew how he and I had met and how he felt about me. He also told her that what drew him to me was that he was intrigued by being with someone who had been called to ministry and just how different and focused I was. However, she was calling me because she was pregnant. Then I understood why God had said no. Eventually I forgave him after we talked about it. It was pretty tumultuous. We went back and forth for eight years. I finally decided that I couldn't keep up with the cycles. Now we're no longer friends.

How has this played out? Well, I've moved on in ministry, and I realize that my life has to be compartmentalized. The work I do at the church is my job. Getting dates is not an issue for me. I typically travel away from my job if I'm going to go out on dates. I had an issue once where one of the church members saw me leaving a diner late with a male friend, and she saw me getting out of his car and into mine. She called my grandmother. It was that big of a deal. So I make sure that the members here never see me out. I have to go far away to go out on dates because people can get so consumed in what they think you're doing that they can't receive you, especially as a female. I don't think that's an issue for men in ministry. Of course, when you're a woman who's thirty-three years old, serving in the capacity that I serve, there always seems to be the question "What is she doing?" Never mind how faithful I serve or the education I have. So I guard against that.

Chapter 7

THE MYTH OF
THE DEADLINE

"You better get married—you don't want those eggs to dry up."

Relationship Status: In a Relationship

Relationship Status: Married

Relationship Status: It's Complicated

Relationship Status: Single

Relationship Status: Trying to Hurry Up!

At the university where I work, there is a phrase that has been adopted over the years called "Ring by Spring." "Ring by spring" reflects the desire that many young college women (mainly at Christian colleges) have during their final year of college: to be engaged by the end of the spring semester before they graduate. If they are engaged by spring, then when they do a graduate, they can begin their adult lives with a partner. Let me start off by saying again that I don't believe there is anything wrong with wanting to partner through life with someone. These are natural desires. However, what has continued to be harmful about the "Ring by Spring" philosophy is that young women pursue relationships during the course of their college career with the intent of getting that ring. Those who have experienced failed relationships or are not in a relationship at all find themselves in a dilemma. They did not reach the deadline. Even though only a small percentage of college couples will be engaged by the end of their last year, this doesn't stop these women from wanting to be a part of that chosen few. This notion is a student tradition that has been passed on for years. While administration and staff have steered clear of adding fuel to the fire, we have not done much to counter it either. "Ring by Spring" has become the butt of jokes as people have begun to realize its ridiculous nature. A recent graduate put it best when she said to me, "We praise the ring by spring, even when we're making fun of it."

I noticed toward the end of last semester there was an increase in senior women whom I encountered who suffered from severe depression because they were not in a relationship or engaged by that time. Many of them wondered what they were possibly going to do with their lives because they were not getting married. They did not understand that they had many options as educated, beautiful women: options like getting a job, or getting an apartment, or traveling, or buying their own things and discovering how and where their gifts and talents fit in this world. I wondered if by not taking an aggressive approach to countering the traditional pressures of the "Ring by Spring" philosophy, were we passively giving a nod to it? It's unfortunate that these women are victims of what so many single people struggle with on a daily basis. It's what I call the myth of the deadline. The myth of the deadline is the idea that there is a particular time in which someone has to be married. It is the idea that there is a point of no return after a certain age. It is reflected in conversations like the one I had with a friend the other day, who looked at me and said, "Oh girl, you're thirty-one—you have time." It was as though my time is running out. It was reflected in an awkward moment I had a few months ago when someone introduced me to another person and started off by saying, "Khristi, this is _____. She got married much, much later in life." I was thrown off, being introduced in a professional setting to a woman who has a PhD by first acknowledging the lateness by which she got married. I'm not sure if she was insulted, but I was.

Many individuals share an overwhelming fear that they will never get married, though most won't admit it. As courageous as I may come off, I have to admit, I have also had this fear—that I'll be one of "those people." I've had to work particularly hard to move past those fears and remind myself that I am never alone. For starters, I'm grateful that I have a family that has never put that kind of pressure on me. My parents have always encouraged me: "You want to be an author? Be an author. You want to move to California? Move to California. You want to be a film-maker? Here's a camera." I have never been made to feel like I am worth any less because I am not a wife. They very rarely ask me about my dating life. They are always curious about who I am as an individual and want me to seek out the very best in life, whether that be through my gifts or my talents. Whenever I have brought a guy home to meet them, they have always been very welcoming. They have always respected my boundaries and only asked me things that were appropriate when I've opened the door for those things to be discussed. I honestly think a lot of the reason for this is because I come from a very colorful family, all having a variety of backgrounds and experiences. I have always had a strong female presence surrounding me, whether it was my grandmothers or my aunts expressing themselves in this world through their freedoms. I have also been blessed to be surrounded by confident men who never felt the need to put my individuality in a box. They have never once suggested that I hurry up and get married. I know of someone whose entire family had serious concerns about the guy she was seeing, but when he proposed to her, her family expressed such joy in the fact that she was finally getting married that it seemed that the marriage proposal outweighed their concerns. She was finally getting married, no matter how harmful the circumstances were. This is an unfortunate attitude that I see in many people within our culture: the attitude that it doesn't matter how it happens, as long as it happens.

Facing Alone

Take a good look at these words. Say them aloud.

> Alone. Abandoned. Lonely. By yourself. Companionless. Deserted. Cat lady/man. Forsaken. Spinster. Hermit. Isolated. Unattended. Unwanted.

At the core of the wound of the single person is the fear of being alone. The words above are blatant fear-mongering terms that are either ingrained in our conscience or spoken by the people around us. While being alone is an adjective used to describe a state that a person is in, it doesn't necessarily insinuate a good or bad thing. However, when it comes to the single person, it is seen as negative. I have tried my very best in this book to put a positive, practical, mission-minded spin on singleness to negate this very idea. For starters, it is a natural reality to desire to do life with someone. The longing for partnership is both biological and beautiful. Whether or not one is in a partnership is both circumstantial and a matter of decisiveness. Because of circumstance, not everyone is in a relationship of their desire, which means that they journey through life as an individual. We have somehow associated that with being a bad thing. While I understand how secular culture views it as bad, I fail to understand why Christian culture has approached it with such contempt and mockery. Jesus was determined to recreate a culture of universal, nontraditional family. Yet centuries later we are hell-bent on categorizing our very own people into molds of tradition-that is, continuously perpetuating the "single is bad" message. Instead of celebrating people growing in their individuality, we chastise them for being lonely.

In a recent conversation with another friend, he shared with me an awkward discussion he had had with a young woman.

> I had a conversation with a couple of friends, and we were talking about marriage and stuff like that. One exchange in particular was with one of my female friends. She said, "God's going to send me my husband, because I desire to be married." So I responded, telling her there was a chance that would not happen. She got so upset. My problem with Christian girls is that they jump the gun. There's nothing wrong with desires and I'm all for it, but marriage isn't everything. Also, everyone is not called to be married. Some people die single. When I tried to remind her of this, she said that she didn't believe that because God said we can have whatever we want. She kept pushing the fact that she was definitely going to get married. I'm not trying to be harsh, but everybody is not supposed to be married, because if that was the case, everyone would die married. I desire to be married, but I'm not seriously considering marriage right now. I am happily single, and I'm not going to rush into anything just to play with a girl's heart. That's basically the message I wanted to send to her. I wanted her to be content in her singleness. If it comes, it comes; if it doesn't, it doesn't.

My friend was coming face-to-face with this young lady's fears as much as he was with her desires. When he suggested that some people die single, I'm sure that frightened her immensely. At the same time, I think she assumed that he meant alone and alone forever, which would not have been my approach to her. For the purposes of my understanding of singleness, that's not how I would have presented it. My friend, however, had come to a place in life where he was content with allowing his life to lead itself. He was unselfish enough to not rush himself or another woman for the sake of making an imagined deadline.

First One to the Finish Line

I once spoke with a woman who told me that one of her friends actually apologized to her for getting engaged first. The woman said that she was floored at her friend's warped way of thinking. She said to me, "She actually thought I cared-like we were in a race or something." One of the problems with the myth of the deadline is that it suggests that we are all in a race to see who will get married first. It implies that those who got married early either did something right or were so blessed to be chosen from among their peers. Those who finish the race later, or worse, never finish the marriage race at all, either did something wrong or are classified as social outcasts.

When I was in seminary, we would take three-hour midterm and final exams. I would always start off calm and collected, but as we neared the timed deadline, I would panic. This was the time when I would make the biggest mistakes. My mentality was to rush the remainder of the questions, trying to finish all of them. My approach was to answer them all as quickly as possible, no matter if I knew the answer or not. This approach never worked for me, and I usually got the majority of those questions wrong. It was the questions at the beginning of the test—the ones I took my time with—that received successful marks. Likewise, many of us feel the pressure to cross the marriage finish line as fast as we can, making rash decisions along the way. The myth of the deadline causes people to rush and not really, truly think things through. I remember when I turned thirty, someone asked me how old I was turning, and when I responded, he said, "Oh my God, girl, you better hurry up and get married." This was a person who was in the middle of a divorce from his second wife and in his late thirties. I thought the situation was quite odd. Had he not been a victim of the mentality behind the myth of the deadline, maybe he could have given me sound advice based on his own diminished circumstances. Instead, that didn't matter because my age was at the forefront. It reflected, again, a very warped way of thinking that we have adopted.

When people rush they typically are prone to making bad decisions. I've seen many failed marriages result from people rushing into an early decision. I've seen many women and men miserable within their marriage because they now look back and realize that they didn't think their decision through. They were so overcome by the pressures to hurry up and get married that they stifled commonsensical thinking processes. I know many women who are so obsessed with having the perfect wedding that they fail to think ahead about what kind of marriage the two will have. I encourage many single people to not fall into this trap. The more people we have prayerfully taking their time in relationships, the more we can prevent wounding outcomes in some of our marriages.

You Don't Have to Fake It

There is an episode of the television show *Sex & the City* called "They Shoot Singles, Don't They?" In that episode the main character Carrie Bradshaw asks, "Has fear of being alone suddenly raised the bar on faking? Are we faking entire relationships? Is it better to fake it than be alone?" In that same episode, in interviews with people on the street, one woman says that she and her boyfriend were compatible except for the fact that he had a specific type of person he preferred physically. After that it appeared as though she dyed her hair, lost weight, and got the necessary plastic surgery procedures in order to look like what he wanted. Another guy said that he couldn't stand his wife and thought she was an idiot. However, he said he could never admit that to her because then she would leave him. The last woman was in a relationship with a man who was hearing-impaired. They could only communicate by sign language. The problem was she didn't know sign language, but evidently it didn't matter because she was in a relationship. In this episode Carrie's friends engage in relationships with guys who are around and convenient to mask their insecurities about being single. All of this was to avoid being alone. They found themselves in a predicament, however, because they had no attraction or connection to any of the men.

Is it better to fake it than to be alone? This is a question I've had to ask myself recently. Because of the myth of the deadline, I have found myself faking it in certain contexts. Someone would show interest in me, and even though I didn't feel like we had a connection, I'd try to overlook that because they had enough of the qualities on my list. I would try my hardest to fake a connection at the expense of my intuition. Some people mistake this as "friend-zoning" the other person. "Friend-zoning" happens when one person communicates that he or she just wants to be friends with the other because he or she doesn't feel a connection. Friend-zoning is often criticized by many, and the person doing the friend-zoning is accused of not giving the other person a chance. Sometimes this is the case. We should open ourselves up to the possibilities of another person beyond our "lists." But if you've opened yourself up to the possibilities for some time and there is still no connection, then you have every right to be honest. We don't have to fake it to avoid being single. I know many people who met a man or a woman and rushed into marriage with someone that they don't even like just because they were tired of people asking them why they weren't married yet. They were tired of being the outcast or not a part of the exclusive marriage club that everyone wants to belong to. They made a rushed decision and now have to live the rest of their lives with that choice.

Desperation, Despair, Depression

The myth of the deadline is fertile ground for desperation. Desperation can cause us to do desperate things, even insomuch that we would do things that might cause personal or emotional harm to ourselves, just for the sake of saying that we have somebody. When a person feels like they are reaching a marital expiration date, irrational behavior and decision making is soon to follow. There are people who—in fear of the approaching deadline—ignored major red flags because they saw no hope beyond that person. There are people who married someone that they just felt lukewarm about in fear that they didn't have time to build a foundation and establish a relationship with someone else by the "deadline." I know of women personally who were intentionally careless in getting pregnant just to distract people from the fact that they are not married. They felt that being mothers would substantiate their identity in this world.

All of this is not without balance. I'm not suggesting that relationships should be perfect before you commit. There will inevitably be circumstantial factors that arise that are not the most ideal. This is where prayer and patience come in. Both parties ought to ask God for wisdom in moving forward in a committed relationship leading to marriage. Don't let your fears turn into desperation, because desperation can cause us to do irrational things. Desperation will always lead to despair. Don't let desperation be your guide. Let love, light, wisdom, and peace be your guides instead.

The myth of the deadline is also fertile ground for depression and anxiety. In the introduction of this book, I mentioned hearing a preacher tell his congregation that single people need to stop being angry with God because they are single. I pointed out that the messages they were receiving from the church might be instigating this anger that single people might be feeling. I'd like to take that one step further by suggesting that when a person feels that they missed a deadline, this brings about automatic feelings of failure. This is when depression can occur. Depression is brought on by feelings of frustration or sadness. Sometimes this depression ensues because of an event or circumstance. The event or circumstance in this case is that they missed the mark and failed to reach a goal. I have counseled many students, clients, and friends who struggle with this. I have had the daunting task of reversing the negative messages they have received stemming from the myth of the deadline. Unfortunately, I've even had to reverse its effects on my own life.

The Waiting Room

One of my favorite movie clips is from the movie *Beetlejuice*. There is a scene when the two main characters are sitting in a waiting room after they died. This scene is hilarious because it is infused with a soundtrack of boring elevator music to drag out the monotony of the waiting. Everyone in the room is already dead, and they not only look dead but it's clear that many of them have been waiting a very long time to move forward with the next steps after their life. The main character looks over at her husband and asks, "Is this what happens when you die?" That is the picture I get when someone suggests to me that I am merely a woman waiting to be found. A picture of a bunch of single people in one room, all looking dead, being serenaded with boring elevator music, and waiting our turn. Is this what happens when you're single and waiting?

There are books and conferences all centered around the topic of what to do while you're waiting, as though we are metaphorically sitting in a waiting room, finding things to do while we pass the time. As a result of that constant message, I fooled myself into waiting around to be found. I wondered why no one had yet found me so that I could start my real life. The notion that we are merely men and women in waiting is a bit misinformed. None of us really know what we're waiting for, how long we're going to be waiting, and if what we're waiting for will ever manifest itself in our life. It also implies that we are somehow stunted in our lives until we get married. It implies that we are incapable of really moving forward in our lives and that life occurs only after marriage. Evangelist and world-renowned speaker Joyce Meyer has a book called *Enjoying Where You Are on the Way to Where You Are Going*. I fell in love with this title as much as I am in love with the book itself. She encourages us that life is not about putting everything into our circumstances but rather in how we approach life through our attitudes. Her overall thesis asked the question, why wait to start to enjoy life? We can enjoy it now. While her book is not for single people specifically, this is a much healthier approach in terms of guiding one through life's journey. There is no such thing as "while you're waiting." You live life regardless. You explore and stretch yourself into new ways of thinking and growing. Life does not begin AFTER you get married. Life begins right now. Don't let it pass you by merely waiting.

There Is No Deadline

> "To everything there is a *season*,
> A time for every purpose under heaven."
> Ecclesiastes 3:1

There is no such thing as a deadline; to everything there is a season. Life is about preparation for the next season and the next season, and so on and so forth. In an effort to highlight the importance of family, Christian culture has inadvertently prearranged a deadline by which single individuals should be married. In order to move away from this, we must rid ourselves of all deadline-oriented language. Just as I suggested in the beginning of the chapter in reference to countering the "Ring by Spring" culture at my school, I also believe that we must devise intentional efforts around countering the myth of the deadline. We need to change our language, phrases, jokes, and assumptions when approaching single people about their journey. If you are single, resist the unrealistic expectations that people attempt to mold you in. Don't allow the system's deadlines to pressure you. People may think you're being sensitive by setting a standard for how you're approached, but don't let that discourage you. In order to shift a culture, it takes an even fiercer approach to overturn it. Like Joyce Meyer wrote, we should encourage each other to enjoy where we are on the way to where we are going. After all, no one except God knows exactly where any of us is headed anyway.

SINCERELY, OVERWHELMED IN AMERICA

For me, more weight as a single person has come from my race. When I moved to America from Nigeria, I realized I was technically "black," so I'm still somewhat naïve with everything because I'm not even technically African American. When I came to America, my first crush was on a white guy, and I didn't even think of him as a white guy. I thought he was just nice to me. When I got to middle school, I liked someone else; and he happened to be white too. So I told him. When I told him, he didn't talk to me at all. I couldn't understand why. I knew he talked to other girls about this. So I was wondering what was wrong with me. I couldn't figure it out. Years later when I got to California, I was talking to a friend about it, and she told me that it could have been because I was black. I never thought about it that way. I had an experience here in California where I liked this guy, and he told me that he wasn't into me because I was black. He was black too, so I was confused. He was more into Latina girls, I guess. I remember freshman year in college I read an article by a guy from another ethnicity that said black women are the least attractive and went through this whole list of psychological and scientific proofs. That was hard for me. There was an interview with Steve Harvey about female black professionals and how a lot of them are gorgeous and single. That made me think: Well, I'm a premed student, I'm a black woman, and I want to be a doctor, and I get scared. This, coupled with the deadline pressure and friends getting married who are around my age-twenty to twenty-two years old-has been overwhelming. It's a lot to take in, and all of it is weighing on me.

American Christian culture is very future-spouse oriented.

I feel like the church in general seems to point to a mission of you finding that one. And messages where we are all together in one space are typically all about traditional family. It can be really awkward, especially if you're someone who is single late in life, and now everyone's asking, "What's wrong with you?" I feel like it's painful for someone to have to sit through that. Sometimes I'm even like, "God, I don't want to be that person."

I wish that American churches were more inclusive in terms of marital status, because there are going to be people who are widowed too and single that way. My mom passed away when I was six years old, and my dad had me and my siblings. I often wonder how that was for him, particularly at that moment being immersed in a very Western culture. Going to church to hear about family and your wife and all that stuff, it wasn't fair for him to not be included. I wish that making it seem like singleness is a disease was not such a big part of American Christian culture. I wish that it wasn't so one-sided. I wish that people were more sensitive.

Chapter 8

THE MYTH OF
THE END ALL, BE ALL

"Don't worry, your day will come.
One day you'll be as lucky as me."

In one of the most enlightening conversations I've ever had about dating and marriage, one of my coworkers made a comment to me that stuck in my head long after. He said, "You know, Khristi, many people think that marriage is the end all, be all. That's not quite true. It's the 'be' and just the 'be.'" Even though there was a certain lightheartedness in what he said, he was intentionally sending me a message to counter misconceptions about marriage and the idea that it is the peak of all life. As I've said earlier, life is about the journey of seasons that we all go through. Marriage is just another season, although our culture has heightened it to be the pinnacle of everything one should seek to obtain in life. The message is that this is where life will begin and life will end. When I was a little girl, it was normal to plan my wedding and decide what my bridesmaids' dresses would look like and which church I'd want to get married in. It was normal to see images in cartoons of brides as princesses being whisked away by their Prince Charming. Typically the bride was locked away in a tower or somewhere, waiting to be rescued. These images alluded that young men should look to rescuing a woman through marriage and a woman should look to waiting to be discovered. The Christian community further reinforced these messages, emphasizing married couples as the center of our community. As time goes on, the wedge driven between those who are single and those who are married gets worse. Those who remain single after a certain time are bombarded with questions, jokes, assumptions, and judgment. It's left me to wonder: is there an all-out attack on single people in the Christian community?

To demonstrate just how far the condemnation has gone, I'll pull from a 2004 message given by R. Albert Mohler, president of the Southern Baptist Theological Seminary. In his lecture titled "The Mystery of Marriage," presented at the New Attitude Conference, he suggested that deliberate singleness is a sin because it is a neglect of Christian responsibility. He blamed factors such as immaturity, fear of commitment, and priority to work and career as the basis for this sin. He explained this further in an article called "Looking Back at 'The Mystery of Marriage.'" He says,

> Other problems are closely associated with this delay of marriage. Speaking to this group of Christian young

people—an outstanding group of young Christian disciples and leaders—I pointed to what sociologists now describe as "extended adolescence"—a period of life that now is extended well into the twenties and even early thirties by many young adults, often young men, who have trouble making the transition to adulthood. I urged these young Christians to seize the biblical concept of marriage and all of its glory, to understand that God has set this covenant before them as expectation, and to channel their energies toward getting married, staying married, and showing God's glory in those marriages. I shared with those who attended the conference my concern that this delay—the deliberate putting off of marriage even among some who intend someday to be married—was "the sin I think besets this generation."[xxii]

The foundation of his thought was to discourage frivolous attitudes toward engaging in relationships. In spite of this, he miserably missed the mark in presentation, grace, and basic pastoral understanding. Blaming single people for their singleness, whether it's by circumstance or choice, is religious bullying. He went on to berate singles for not taking marriage seriously, when in all actuality, some may argue that the Christian community takes it way too seriously. Associating any form of singleness with sin is a mockery of Jesus's kingdom principles. These include principles of freedom, wholeness, and inclusion. Unfortunately, even in Mohler's extremeness, he highlighted what is at the core of the anti-single culture we have created within the Christian community. If sin leads to shame and our singleness is perpetually being shamed, then many single people will subconsciously associate their single status with sin. I believe we're seeing the adverse effects of this in our present day.

In her article "Is Singleness a Sin?," Camerin Courtney responds to Mohler's discourse with righteous indignation.

> When Mohler calls marriage the "ultimate priority God has called us to," I cringe. Not because I'm anti-marriage, but because I don't find backing for this in the Bible. I don't see the place where marriage is called a requirement. It's called a blessing many times, but then so is singleness. The only list of Christ-follower requirements I find in my Bible is in Micah 6:8 "He has showed you, O man, what is good. And what does the Lord require of you? To act justly and to love mercy and to walk humbly with your God." These things, not marriage, should be our ultimate priorities.[xxiii]

In spite of Mohler's radical approach, all attacks on singleness don't come in this form. Some people would read what Mohler said and resolve that his seemingly bigoted language is far from their personal views. These are the same people who I would encourage to evaluate how they, too, may have unintentionally encouraged the ostracizing of singles in their communities. For a group of people who lean on Jesus's teaching of anti-condemnation, as a community, we have done a really good job of condemning those who don't fit into our molds. We blame men for not being fervent, powerful leaders, even though men can choose to lead in their own way. We blame women for being too sassy and educated, often concluding that those are the reasons they are alone. Our language can be so harsh and divisive that we leave very little room for grace and understanding. Someone once said that the Christian community multiplies by dividing. With this, has the Christian community discriminated against single people, pushing them farther and farther from the center of acceptance? Perhaps we should revisit the person at the core of singleness: ourself.

Assessment

While I don't believe that people need to be blamed for their singleness, I do believe it's important to practice self-reflection and evaluation. It's important to assess your current state mentally, personally, and emotionally. Self-examination is a commonly overlooked spiritual practice. Typically, it is during the seasons of Lent and Advent that people are encouraged to look inwardly. Nonetheless, self-examination should be a regular practice for everyone. We need to be honest with ourselves about ourselves so that we can be better people for our community, family, and friendships as well as romantic relationships. In self-assessment you ask yourself all of the hard questions. You open yourself up for God to guide you into areas of improvement. You make yourself aware of how you navigate through the world. I've included a few questions below to help you get started on your personal assessment.

1) **What is your perception of yourself? Are you confident in your individuality? Why or why not?**

_____

_____

_____

_____

_____

2) **Describe your personality. (Consider taking the Myers-Briggs Personality Assessment, which can be located online.)**

_____

_____

_____

_____

_____

3) **Has your character ever been criticized? Do you believe it was justified? Why or why not?**

_____

_____

_____

_____

_____

4) What are your greatest strengths? What are your
   weaknesses?

_____

_____

_____

_____

_____

5) How can you capitalize and invest in your strengths?
   What kinds of activities can you engage in to nurture those areas?

_____

_____

_____

_____

_____

6) How can you invest and work on your weaknesses?
   How can you actively pursue growth in those areas?

_____
_____
_____
_____
_____

7) What is your mission statement in life?

_____
_____
_____
_____
_____

8) Are you content in your singleness? Why or why not?

_____
_____
_____
_____
_____

9) How are you living out your call to singleness? (If you are in a relationship, how are you living out your call to singleness within your relationship?)

_____
_____
_____

_____

_____

Take some time to reflect on your answers to these questions. They are just the beginning of making a strong assessment of one's self. The gift of self-awareness is one of the greatest lessons I have ever discovered. Only then can you move toward determining how you can successfully navigate within the context of a relationship.

Acceptance

One of the greatest obstructions of forward movement is denial. Another is resentment. Unfortunately many of us find ourselves in spaces that conflict with our desires, and we are left with feelings of denial and resentment. I hate it when people tell me that I should accept the rejection of my wants. I never understood why I should have to accept anything less than what my heart desires. In turn, the concept of "the will of God" has always perplexed me. We are told that we must accept the will of God, despite the fact that sometimes the will of God doesn't always agree with our human longings. Sometimes our longings are blatantly not good for us. But what about the longings that are? Why should I be withheld from those good things and then told to just accept it? Many times, without conversation, patience, and understanding, people are told that they should just accept where they are. I have never understood that approach. Acceptance is not an easy process. One cannot wave a magic wand or blink their eyes and step into it. Therefore, phrases like "Get over it," "Stop being angry about being single," and "Just accept it" are not constructive or helpful. They actually do more harm than good, and they typically come from people who lack sensitivity and the skills to empathize. Still, we have to begin to guide ourselves and to guide others into walking into the reality of our lives. This is inevitably an uncomfortable process, but it is a necessary one. Whether you are single by choice, single by circumstance, or widowed or divorced, the process of acceptance awaits you. Someone once said "Let reality be reality. Let things flow naturally forward." That's the direction that we should strive to move in life: forward. Acceptance is about forward movement and being courageous enough to hope.

I believe a major reason for any hesitancy in acceptance is because we've failed to accept that, in spite of our uncomfortable realities, God has a plan and an even better reality that God is working out on our behalf. There is a passage in Romans 8:28 that says, "And we know that all things work together for good to them that love God, to them who are the called according to his purpose." I've been quoting that scripture since my childhood in Sunday school. It's been the theme for many conferences and revivals. I've come to realize that all things aren't just working, but they are connecting. Every single thing that has happened, the good and the bad, God is somehow finding ways to connect. God works tirelessly to redeem all things back to God's-self. God works earnestly to put all the pieces of our puzzle together and somehow make them fit into someone else's puzzle to cause a domino effect of healing and wholeness. It may not be easy to accept life, but our hope is that God is using who we are in our present to connect to a greater future.

A Commitment to Singleness

Singleness is not just a state of default; living out your singleness is a commitment. It's a commitment to honor and value the person God invested love in—you. Naturally we need to live our lives fearing God and pursuing wisdom. Whatever you choose to pursue, whether that's relationships or career or passions, is your prerogative. Just make sure whatever you do, you don't leave yourself out in the process. Pursue things that bring you life and stay away from the things you feel pressured or intimidated into doing. Life is so unpredictable. We can't afford to spend it being tied down by oppressive systems. Rid yourselves of stereotypes and misconceptions. Rid yourself of having to give an account for why you are where you are in life. Refuse to be on the tail end of someone else's joke. Reject people's need to condemn you for your individuality. We have to fight for our right to pursue the fullness of life, to pursue peace, and to pursue hope.

Commit to your singleness as much as you would commit to anything or anyone else. Why? Because you want to be the best possible person you can be for yourself. If by some chance you meet a life partner along the way, you will furthermore want to be the best for him or her as well. You want to be the best possible person you can be for any future children you may have. You want to be the best coworker, friend, son, daughter, neighbor, sister, or brother. You should want to be the best you: whole, happy, and healthy.

SINCERELY,
ME

"The kingdom of heaven is like treasure hidden in a field. When a man found it, he hid it again, and then in his joy went and sold all he had and bought that field."

Matthew 13:44

For my entire life I've been in search of something special. I've looked for it in everything from friendships, relationships with men, institutions, and educational degrees. It's taken a long time for me to realize that what I was looking for was literally staring at me in the mirror. In the passage of scripture above, Jesus says there was a man who was looking in a field and found a treasure hidden within it. When he found the treasure, he hid it again and then went and sold everything he had, not just to buy the treasure, but to buy the field too. He bought all of the dirt and weeds and thorns and stones that came with that treasure! Why didn't he just go for the treasure itself? Why did he feel that all of those other seemingly worthless things were worth buying too? To the man, everything was worth investing in. When I read it, I immediately inserted myself into that story. As the person looking for the treasure, I had found what I was looking for in myself. I was not only the person looking for the treasure, but I was that treasure as well. I wondered if I'd invested too much in only the valuable qualities and neglected the dirty field that came along with me. One day I woke up and realized just how selfish I was. I am selfish with myself. I hide my talents and let them out when I feel like it. I take all my pains, and I keep them hidden deep inside, never allowing anyone else to learn from those experiences. I take my celebrations and success and share them with my chosen few. That's not noble; it's selfish. People need to hear our stories.

There was also another person who took the place of the man discovering the treasure in the field. That person was Jesus. Jesus invested in me to not only give up his entire life to purchase the parts of me that are good and acceptable; he purchased the areas of weakness and darkness as well. I've been reluctant to take his lead in purchasing my entire field. There are stories and lessons and deep, dark, complicated spaces in my mind and heart that I have deliberately chosen to keep hidden. But those areas are important and ultimately can help somebody else, so I—like the man and like Jesus before me—have chosen to commit myself to selling everything I have to buy my entire field.

Are you willing to do the same? Are you hiding the treasure that is yourself out of fear that who you are is not enough? It doesn't matter where you may find yourself in life, whether single, married, divorced, or widowed: invest in your entire field for no other reason other than the fact that you're worth it.

ENDNOTES

i   Accumulation Theory. *University of Oregon.* http://pages.
     uoregon.edu/dmerskin/theories.htm

ii   Noling, Jamie. 2013. "Singleness: More Than a Holding
     Pattern." *Results May Vary. Christian Women Reflect on
     Post-College Life.* (pp. 37-45). San Diego, CA: Point Loma
     Press.

iii Beaty, Katelyn. "Same-Sex Marriage and the Single
     Christian. How marriage-happy churches are unwittingly
     fueling same-sex coupling—and leaving singles like me
     in the dust." *Christianity Today.* 1 July 2013. http://www.
     christianitytoday.com/ct/2013/july-web-only/same-sex-
     marriage-and-single-christian.html

iv   Rodney Clapp, *Families at the Crossroads* (Downers Grove,
     Ill: InterVarsity Press, 1993), p. 89.

v   Rodney Clapp, *Families at the Crossroads* (Downers Grove,
     Ill: InterVarsity Press, 1993), p. 91, 92.

vi   Rodney Clapp, *Families at the Crossroads* (Downers Grove,
     Ill: InterVarsity Press, 1993), p. 113.

vii   Holy Bible, Exodus Ch. 32

viii   Holy Bible, Luke Ch. 20 NIV

ix   http://www.thefreedictionary.com/Individual+freedom

x   Holy Bible, Genesis Ch. 1

xi   Anne, Libby. "What I Learned From Joshua Harris." *Love, Joy, Feminism.* 25 October 2012. http://www.patheos.com/blogs/lovejoyfeminism/2012/10/what-i-learned-from-joshua-harris.html

xii   "My Husband Is Not My Soul Mate." *The Art in Life.* 22 July 2013. http://theartinlife.wordpress.com/2013/07/22/my-husband-is-not-my-soul-mate/

xiii   Kristoff, Nicolas D., & WuDunn, Sheryl. *Half the Sky* (New York: Vintage Books, 2010), p. 6.

xiv   Rodney Clapp, *Families at the Crossroads* (Downers Grove, Ill: InterVarsity Press, 1993), p. 100.

xv   http://dictionary.reference.com/browse/purity

xvi   "The Courage to Be" was a phrase coined by theologian Paul Tillich as the title of one of many of his books.

xvii   David G. Benner, *The Gift of Being Yourself* (Downers Grove, Ill: InterVarsity Press, 2004), p. 20.

xviii   Katelyn Beaty, *Same-Sex Marriage & the Single Christian*

xix   Holy Bible, Exodus-Numbers

xx   Fileta, Debra K. "What Not to Say to Singles: Rethinking 3 phrases often used to encourage singles." *Relevant Magazine.* 17 July 2013. http://www.relevantmagazine.com/life/relationships/what-not-say-singles

xxi   David G. Benner, *The Gift of Being Yourself* (Downers
       Grove, Ill: InterVarsity Press, 2004), p. 58.

xxii   Mohler, Albert. "Looking Back at the Mystery of
       Marriage, Part 1." *AlbertMohler.com*. 19 August
       2004. http://www.albertmohler.com/2004/08/19/
       looking-back-at-the-mystery-of-marriage-part-one/

xxiii Courtney, Camerin. "Is Singleness a Sin?" *Crosswalk*. 11
       August 2004. http://www.crosswalk.com/11621125/?p=3

Made in the USA
San Bernardino, CA
19 November 2013